WORLD BANK WORKING PAPER NO. 87

I0119789

Development of Capital Markets and Institutional Investors in Russia

Recent Achievements and Policy Challenges Ahead

Michel Noel
Zeynep Kantur
Evgeny Krasnov
Sue Rutledge

THE WORLD BANK
Washington, D.C.

World Bank Working Papers are published to communicate the results of the Bank's work to the development community with the least possible delay. The manuscript of this paper therefore has not been prepared in accordance with the procedures appropriate to formally-edited texts. Some sources cited in this paper may be informal documents that are not readily available.

ISBN-10: 0-8213-6794-3   ISBN-13: 978-0-8213-6794-0
eISBN: 0-8213-6795-1
ISSN: 1726-5878   DOI: 10.1596/978-0-8213-6794-0

Michel Noel is Lead Financial Specialist in the Private & Financial Sectors Development Sector unit of Europe and Central Asia Region of the World Bank. Zeynep Kantur is Financial Sector Specialist in the Financial Sector Operations & Policy Department of the World Bank. Evgeny Krasnov is Financial Analyst in the Moscow office of the World Bank. Sue Rutledge is Senior Private Sector Development Specialist in the Private & Financial Sectors Development Sector unit of Europe and Central Asia Region of the World Bank.

Library of Congress Cataloging-in-Publication Data

Development of capital markets and institutional investors in Russia : recent
achievements and policy challenges ahead/Michel Noel . . . [et al.].
     p. cm.—(World Bank working paper ; no. 87)
  Includes bibliographical references and index.
  ISBN-13: 978-0-8213-6794-0 (alk. paper)
  ISBN-10: 0-8213-6794-3 (alk. paper)
  ISBN-10: 0-8213-6795-1 (electronic : alk. paper)
  1. Capital market—Russia (Federation) 2. Finance–Russia (Federation)
3. Russia (Federation)—Economic Policy. I. Noel, Michel, 1954–HG5580.2.A3D49 2006
    332¢.04150947—dc22   2006020560

Contents

LIST OF TABLES

LIST OF FIGURES

LIST OF BOXES

Acknowledgments

This Report was prepared by a Task Team led by Michel Noel (Lead Financial Specialist, ECSPF), Zeynep Kantur (Financial Sector Specialist, OPD), Evgeny Krasnov (Financial Analyst, ECSPF—Moscow Office) and Sue Rutledge (Senior Private Sector Development Specialist, ECSPF). The Task Team consisted of Rupa Bhattasali (Consultant, ECSPF), Steen Byskov (Consultant, ECSPF), Pasquale di Benedetta (Consultant, ECSPF), Yumi Ejiri (Consultant, ECSPF), and Dan Goldblum (Financial Sector Specialist, OPD).

The Team extends special thanks to Kristalina Georgieva (Country Director, ECCU1), Fernando Montes-Negret (Director, ECSPF), Tunc Uyanik (Sector Manager, ECSPF) and Yasuo Izumi (Program Manager, PA9SS) for their guidance and support in the preparation of the Report. The Team is grateful to Paula Perttunen (Lead Financial Specialist, ECSPF) for agreeing to be Team Advisor and for her very useful comments on an earlier version of the Report. The Team is grateful to Claire Grose (Senior Financial Specialist, OPD), Yibin Mu (Financial Economist, OPD) and Alexander Morozov (Senior Economist, ECSPE—Moscow Office) for agreeing to be Peer Reviewers for the Report. The Team is thankful to Claire Grose, Alexander Morozov, Luigi Passamonti (Senior Advisor, OPD), and Dmitri Vittas (Senior Advisor, OPD), for their very useful comments on an early version of the Report. The Team is also grateful to Sylvie Bossoutrot (Senior Operations Officer, ECSPF) for her invaluable collaboration in the framework the Russia Capital Market Development Project.

Alberto Monti, Tyge Rasmussen, Lorenzo Savorelli, and Paul Sullivan (Consultants, ECSPF) all provided invaluable inputs to the Report.

The field visits took place in November 2003 and April–May 2004. The updates of the finding of the mission were done by Moscow based consultants at the end of 2004 and end of 2005. The Report was prepared in consultation with the Central Bank of Russia, the Ministry of Finance, the Federal Commission on Securities Markets, the Federal Financial Market Service, the Center for Capital Market Development (CCMD), the Federal Insurance Supervision Service, the Ministry of Economic Development and Trade, the National Association of Market Participants (NAUFOR), the National Stock Market Association (NFA), the Moscow Interbank Currency Stock Exchange (MICEX), the Russian Trading System (RTS), the National Depository Center (NDC), the Depository and Clearing Center (DCC), the All Russia Insurance Union (ARIA), the Non-State Pension Fund Inspection, National Association of Asset Management Companies (NLU), as well as major Russian and foreign owned banks, investment companies, insurance/reinsurance firms, mutual funds and pension funds.

The Team would like to express their gratitude to the Russian government officials who received the World Bank mission, and generously gave their time to share their knowledge and insights on the prospects for future market development. The authors are grateful to the staff of the Center for Capital Market Development (CCMD) for taking time to discuss the key policy recommendations of the Report. The authors are also grateful to private sector counterparts who shared valued information on market development both during and following the World Bank missions.

Abbreviations

ADR	American depositary receipt
AIF	Corporate investment fund
AMC	Asset Management Company
bp	Basis points
CBR	Central Bank of Russia
CCS	Central clearing system
CD	Central depository
CPSS	Committee on Payment and Settlement Systems
CSD	Central settlement depository
CSS	Central settlement system
DIS	Deposit insurance system
DVP	Delivery versus payment
EU	European Union
FCSM	Federal commission for securities market
FIG	Financial industrial group
FISS	Federal insurance supervision service
FSFM	Federal financial market service
GDP	Gross domestic product
GDR	Global depositary receipt
GOR	Government of Russian Federation
IAIS	International association of insurance supervisors
IAS	International accounting standard
IFRS	International financial reporting standards
IOSCO	International Organization of Securities Commissions
IPO	Initial public offering
LSE	London stock exchange
MICEX	Moscow inter-bank currency exchange
MOF	Ministry of Finance
MSE	Moscow stock exchange
MTPL	Motor third party liability
NAV	Net asset value
NSPF	Non-state pension fund
NYSE	New York stock exchange
OECD	Organization for Economic Cooperation and Development
OFZ	Government bond
OTC	Over the counter
PFR	Pension Fund of Russia
PIF	Unit investment fund
RF	Russian Federation
RTS	Russian trading system
Rub	Russian Ruble
RTGS	Real time gross settlement

RTS	Russian trading system
SELT	System of electronic lot trades in currency
SF	Subject of the Federation
US$	US Dollar
UTS	Unified trading system
SPV	Special Purpose Vehicle
YTM	Yield to maturity

Executive Summary

Capital Market and Institutional Investors: Recent Evolution

Rapid Economic Growth and Macroeconomic Stability Since the 1998 Crisis Have Led to Steady Monetization of the Economy and Expansion of the Banking Sector, Although the Latter Remains Structurally Unbalanced

Following the 1998 crisis, the Russian economy expanded at an average 6 percent per year while monetary and fiscal policies resulted in a drop in inflation (11–12 percent in 2003–05) and growing budget surpluses peaking at 7 percent of GDP in 2005. At the same time, monetization of the economy proceeded at a rapid pace, with the ratio of M2 to GDP growing from 19 percent by end of 1995 to 31.6 by end of 2004, slightly declining to 27.9 percent by end 2005, and banking assets as a share of GDP grew from 32.9 percent by end 2000 to 45 percent by end 2005. However, the banking sector remains highly concentrated in Moscow. With one dominant state-owned bank, a handful of medium to large money center banks and a plethora of pocket banks, the structure of the sector is unbalanced, reducing both its resilience and its ability to serve the needs of the economy.

The Domestic Government Bond (OFZ) Market Has Re-Emerged Slowly Over the Last Five Years. By Contrast, the Sub-Sovereign and Corporate Bond Markets Have Developed Vigorously, with the Moscow Bond as Benchmark

As a result of budget surpluses over the last five years, government bond (OFZ) issuance has been limited to the refinancing of the domestic and external debt, as well as restructuring of the terms of the debt portfolio. In addition, CBR has been able to sell a major portion of its portfolio on the secondary market. As a result, while total OFZ outstanding grew from Rub506.1 billion by end 2000 to Rub851.1 billion (US$29.5 billion) by end 2005, the OFZ in circulation grew from Rub230 billion (45 percent of the total outstanding) by end 2000 to Rub721.6 billion (85 percent of the total outstanding) by end 2005. Overall, over two thirds of the demand for OFZs originates from state-related institutions under buy and hold strategies. As a result, secondary market liquidity is severely limited, and market participants do not regard the OFZ yield curve as a market benchmark. By contrast, the sub-sovereign bond market has grown vigorously since its re-emergence in 2001 and has now become the largest sub-sovereign bond market among emerging economies with Rub161 billion (equivalent to US$5.6 billion) bonds outstanding. Secondary market liquidity has increased substantially, but remains concentrated on Moscow and St Petersburg issues. The Moscow bond has emerged as the benchmark for the sub-sovereign and corporate bond markets. The corporate bond market grew from Rub39 billion by end 2000 to Rub481 billion by end 2005 (equivalent of US$16.7 billion). By end of 2005, the corporate bond market comprised over 310 bonds issued by over 220 companies. Corporate bonds are the most liquid in the secondary market with the most diversified investor base.

The turnover in corporate bonds and of blue chip sub-sovereign bonds (Moscow, St. Petersburg, and Moscow Oblast) far exceeds the turnover in government securities.

*Equity Market Capitalization Has Expanded Rapidly Over the Last Five Years,
But the Market is Under Growing Competition From Offshore Equity Issuance
and Trading*

Equity market capitalization has expanded rapidly over the last five years, reaching over
US$500 billion by end-2005, or about 70 percent of GDP. Starting in 2005, capitalization
expanded both as a result of appreciation and of increase in stocks admitted to trading, which
grew from 215 at the end of 2004 to 277 at the end of 2005. However, the market remains highly
concentrated in terms of volume and trading among the top 5–10 dozen issuers, mostly in oil,
gas, electricity, metals, and telecoms sectors. In 2003–2004, secondary trading in Russian securities began to shift to international markets causing major concern of the Russian securities
market regulator. The shift in liquidity was partially caused by the perceived high transaction
cost and higher ownership risk of local trading by international institutional investors. In
2004–05, there was a wave of Russian IPOs, but most of them were done through international
markets placement of ADRs, GDRs, and SPVs, primarily on London Stock Exchange (LSE).

*Institutional Investors Have Grown Substantially Over the Past Five Years But
the Sector Remains Dominated by Own-Investment Plays by Large
Corporations and by Tax Avoidance Schemes*

The growth of the investment fund industry has been led by closed-end funds established
by corporations as investment and tax saving schemes. Non-state pension funds (NSPFs)
investments are largely dominated by equity, in particular stock of the parent company,
indicating that many NSPFs have been established to provide financing for large enterprise
investments. Until recently, a significant share of voluntary life and property insurance constituted of tax avoidance schemes such as wage schemes. The introduction of new capital
requirements is expected to lead to a consolidation in the sector, with large companies
leaving the gray market.

Securities Markets: Key Impediments For Further
Development and Policy Challenges Ahead

The Legal and Regulatory Framework for Securities Market
is Incomplete and Fragmented

The legal and regulatory framework for the securities market suffers from major gaps,
including the absence of a legal base for derivatives, deficiencies in exchange trade regulations the absence of effective penalties for insider trading and price manipulation, absence
of protection of investors against abusive takeover practices, and absence of legal and regulatory framework for securitization.

To Address These Issues, FSFM is Focusing on a Number of Priority Actions

As of the beginning 2006, the FSFM is focusing on the following legal initiatives:

■ Adoption of the Law on the Central Depositary, which should strengthen the domestic market infrastructure competitiveness.

■ Adoption of the Law on Derivatives with necessary amendments to the civil code to provide legal protection for derivatives transaction.

■ Adoption of the Exchange Trading Regulation to increase competitiveness of Russian capital market infrastructure.

■ Adoption of the Law on Inside Information and Market Manipulation to raise confidence in Russian capital market.

■ Adoption of clear regulation of corporate mergers as step towards more civilized stock market and better investment climate.

■ Adoption of legislation on securitization to create new financial instruments and investment opportunities for capital market investors.

Over the medium-term, it would be advisable to restructure this framework into fewer but mutually consistent legislative acts, focusing laws on general regulatory principles and leaving detailed regulations for specific regulatory acts that can be amended more easily.

The Infrastructure For Securities Markets Suffers From Serious Deficiencies, and FSFM is Taking Measures to Address Them

The development of the securities market is hampered by deficiencies in market infrastructure, including: (i) high degree of market fragmentation, with several markets competing with each other and offering their own settlement and clearing procedures; (ii) high registrar risk; (iii) low adaptability of record keeping system to foreign registration and settlement systems; (iv) high cost of pre-deposit funds and pre-funding and high risk on non-payment under free delivery method; (v) absence of RTGS; and (vi) low transparency of OTC market.

FSFM is focusing on key measures to address these deficiencies:

■ Establishing the CSD system, amending the law on clearing to introduce centralized settlement and clearing, and capitalizing the system.

■ Ensuring that effective RTGS is in place, at least on MICEX and RTS; enabling DVP to replace pre-depositing and pre-funding system.

■ Improving registrars system through consolidation of existing registrars, adopting international best practices for risk control (CPSS/IOSCO among others), evaluating the linkage between CSD and the registrars, and evaluating CSD as registrar for listed securities.

The Development of the Government Bond Market is Hampered by Several Impediments, and the Government can Take Key Measures to Address Them

The development of the Government bond market faces a number of impediments, including:

(i) High concentration of government debt in buy and hold portfolios

(ii) Absence of primary dealer (PD) system

(iii) Fragmentation of the portfolio, although MOF has established a placement schedule and created "benchmark" issues

(iv) Restrictions on non-resident investing in Russia's capital market (supposed to be lifted from January 1, 2007)

As a result of the impediments above Government bond market lacks liquidity and OFZ yields are not indicative of real interest rates on the market.

To overcome existing impediments, the government could undertake the following measures:

- Implement a primary dealer system.
- Prepare to face additional demand for OFZs following the removal of restrictions on non-resident investing in OFZs.
- Take into account additional demand coming from new pension savings.
- Continue to develop the placement schedule and maintain the "benchmark" issue of certain size and duration.

The Implementation of the Legal and Regulatory Framework for the Sub-Sovereign Bond Market is Encountering Difficulties, Which the Government Can Address Through a Series of Key Measures

A significant number of Subjects of the Federation (SFs) broke their budget deficit limit and their debt exposure limit since 2000. Budget loans intended to cover short-term liquidity gaps of SFs are becoming an instrument to finance structural deficits of several SFs. Controls on prudential limits on guarantees by SFs cannot be exercised in the absence of reliable data on SF guarantees. SFs are in some cases shareholders of regional banks that can make loans to them. And the procedures for intervention by higher levels of the Federal system in case of debt default by a sub-sovereign entity remain vague.

The authorities can take a number of key measures to address these difficulties. These include:

- Enforce prudential limits by denying approvals for bond issuance for SFs and municipalities in breach of these limits.
- Include past due payments in calculation of indebtedness limits.
- Enforce repayment of existing budget loans and other Federal debts within the fiscal year.
- Eliminate new related party borrowing from affiliated banks, and adopt standards for competitive selection for bank creditors and bond underwriters.
- Adopt law on bankruptcy of regions and municipalities, substituting for current provisions on sub-sovereign debt default in the Budget Code.

Market Risk is Increasing on the Corporate Bond Market, and the Authorities are Already Taking, and Plan to Undertake Further Measures to Reduce This Risk

The authorities are taking a number of measures to improve the extent and quality of disclosure by listed corporations, including: (i) encouraging listed corporations to adopt IAS; (ii) improve governance of listed corporations through the adoption of the corporate governance code; and (iii) establish differential corporate requirements in MICEX and RTS listing categories, on the basis of self-declaration.

Going forward, the authorities could focus on the following actions:

- Adopt a realistic calendar for the adoption of new listing rules including IAS requirement for listing on MICEX and RTS.
- Require listed companies to disclose their ultimate economic beneficiaries.
- Adopt specific Governance Code criteria and enforce their implementation by listed companies.

The Development of the Equities Market is Subject to a Number of Supply-Side and Demand-Side Constraints, Which the Authorities Can Address Through Specific actions

On the supply side, the development of the market is constrained by corporate preference towards owner control within a small closed group, and a reluctance to operate companies as publicly traded entities. Financial industrial groups (FIGs) tend to favor diversification through control and integration of other companies rather than through diversified portfolio of traded securities. Large companies tend to place IPOs abroad and medium-size companies may feel too small to access the domestic market on their own or may be reluctant to access the market for fear of abusive takeover practices. On the demand side, broad participation by domestic investors is impeded by absence of effective legal base for prevention against manipulation and unfair market practices. Rapid increase in the share of Russian equity turnover on foreign exchanges results from inefficiencies in market infrastructure and high transactions costs on domestic exchanges.

The authorities can take a number of key actions to address these constraints:

- Adopt legislation on insider trading and price manipulation.
- Improve regulation of hostile takeover.
- Establish CD, introduce centralized settlement and clearing system.
- Allow foreign securities trading though RDRs on MICEX and RTS.
- Adopt calendar for IAS reporting for listed companies.
- Enforce Governance Code criteria for listed companies.

Institutional Investors: Key Impediments to Further Development and Policy Challenges Ahead

Several Deficiencies Hamper the Development of the Investment Fund Industry, Which the Authorities Can Address Through a Number of Practical Actions

Under the Investment Funds Law, FSFM enforcement powers over the investment fund industry are limited. Although FSFM can impose sanctions against market participants under the Administrative Code, fines are insufficient. Though FSFM can suspend distribution of shares over a six-months period, it has no authority to revoke the license of a registered management company or investment trust. The Law does not contain any provisions, which would hold natural persons working for an entity liable for violations of the Law. The Law does not provide sufficient investigation authority to FSFM to properly monitor the industry. While FSFM has access to fund books and records, it cannot question third parties that are often critical to any securities investigations. Although the Law prohibits a depository, registrar, auditor or appraiser of the assets of the joint-stock investment fund from also being a shareholder in the fund, it does not prohibit a third entity, such as a financial conglomerate, from being a controlling shareholder in both entities. The same applies to employees of the above entities.

The authorities can take a number of measures to address these deficiencies:

- Strengthen enforcement powers of FSFM over investment funds and fund management companies, including authority to annul licenses and authority to apply fines.
- Strengthen investigative powers of FSFM over funds, fund management companies and registrars.
- Establish provisions holding natural persons liable for violations of the Law, acting individually or on behalf of a legal entity (fund, fund management company).
- Strengthen independence between financial conglomerates and their employers and joint stock investment funds, unit investment funds, fund depositories, registrars and auditors.

The Development of Non-State Pension Funds Suffers From Major Impediments, Which the Authorities Can Address Through Specific Measures

The development of non-state pension funds (NSPFs) suffers from three major impediments. First, NSPFs are insufficiently regulated and supervised. A large number of NSPFs are company plans run by large employers as a source of financing for company shares and investments, rather than as mechanisms to optimize returns for beneficiaries while minimizing risks. Market-based pension funds are limited in number. Second, the legal and regulatory framework for NSPFs does not adequately protect contributors' rights, in particular non-discrimination in access, vested rights, and portability. Third, the vast majority of the population is unaware of NSPF activities and the confidence level of those who are aware of their activities is predictably low.

The authorities can address these impediments by taking key measures:

- Strengthen regulation and supervision of NSPFs in accordance with international standards.
- Establish and enforce comprehensive disclosure rules for NSPFs.
- Strictly limit the share of NSPF portfolio that can be invested in the NSPF founding company.

The Development of the Insurance Sector Faces a Number of Major Impediments

The development of the insurance sector faces a number of major impediments, including: (i) lack of separation between life and non-life insurance; (ii) undercapitalization of insurance companies; (iii) limited capacity to carry out actuarial assessment of reserves; (iv) difficulties in implementing compulsory motor third party liability insurance (MTPL);

(v) limitations to foreign participation in the sector; (vi) absence of consumer protection rules; (vi) weaknesses in the legal and regulatory framework for insurance undertakings, in particular financial dependence of the new Federal Insurance Supervision Service (FISS) from MOF, lack of enforcement powers of FISS, and lack of oversight over reinsurance activities and over investment activities of insurance companies.

The Authorities Can Take a Number of Practical Measures to Address These Impediments

Priority measures are:

- Strengthen coordination between FISS, MOF and FSFM.
- Strictly enforce minimum capital requirements.
- Grant FISS the power to check fitness and propriety of qualified shareholders, controllers and beneficial owners of insurance companies at licensing/re-licensing stage, and to approve subsequent changes in control of supervised entities.
- Strengthen monitoring by FISS of investment activities and changes in investment portfolio of insurance undertakings.
- Establish clear anti-money laundering procedures, and grant FISS the power to review reinsurance policies of supervised entities.
- Establish rules on supplemental supervision of insurance companies belonging to insurance groups or financial conglomerates.
- Require insurance companies to have an internal audit function.
- Enact consumer protection rules.

CHAPTER 1

Capital Markets and Institutional Investors: Recent Evolution

The Favorable Macroeconomic Environment Has Led to Increased
Monetization of the Economy. However, Banking Sector Assests
Still Remain Low by International Standards

Since the 1998 crisis, the Russian economy expanded at an average rate of 6 percent per year, while tight monetary and fiscal policies in highly favorable macroeconomic environsus oil revenues and ruble appreciation against the US$enabled the Russian Federation to reduce its debt/GDP ratio from over 100 percent in 1999 to 12 percent by the end of 2005. As a result of these positive developments, the credit rating of the Russian Federation was raised from CCC+ at the beginning of 2000 to BBB at the end of 2005. The spreads on government Eurobonds have narrowed considerably: EMBI + Russia index has dropped from average 1170 bps in December 2000 to average 115 bps in December 2005.

The monetization of the Russian economy proceeded at a rapid pace since the 1998 crisis, with M2/GDP growing from 20.6 percent by end 1999 to 31.6 percent by end 2004, declining slightly to 27.9 percent by end 2005. However, this growth is attributed to growing demand for real money balances by the private sector rather than increase in efficiency of financial intermediation.

At the same time, banking assets as a share of GDP grew from 32.9 percent by end 1999 to 45 percent by end 2005, with rapid credit growth in energy and construction sectors and in consumer lending. The sector is highly concentrated in Moscow, with nearly 80 percent of private enterprise deposits and 60 percent of government deposits placed in Moscow-based banks, and enterprises located in Moscow receiving about half of total bank loans to the corporate sector. With one dominant state-owned bank, a handful of medium to large money center banks and a plethora of small pocket banks, the structure of the sector is

1

unbalanced reducing both the resilience of the system and its ability to serve the needs of the economy. Credit risk is a concern given rapid credit growth and concentrated loan exposures, particularly to related parties. Increased competition is putting downward pressure on interest margins while increased cost and recent decline in trading income further erode banks' profitability.

The Domestic Government Bond Market Has Re-emerged Slowly Following the 1998 Crisis, But the OFZ Yield Curve is Not Regarded as a Market Benchmark by Investors

The domestic government bond market has re-emerged slowly following the 1998 crisis. Domestic government debt in form of government bonds (OFZ) grew from Rub506.1 billion by end of 2000 to Rub851.1 billion by end of 2005. At the same time, the OFZ in circulation (excluding CBR portfolio) grew from Rub228 billion by end 2000 (45 percent of the OFZs outstanding) to Rub721.6 billion by end 2005 (85 percent of the OFZs outstanding). The share of OFZ traded on the secondary market has doubled as CBR has restructured and sold the major portion of its portfolio on the open market. In relation to GDP, OFZ in circulation accounted for about 3.3 percent by end 2005. Thanks to high oil prices and tight fiscal stance, the government has run budget surpluses over the last five years and new bond issuance has been limited to refinancing of domestic debt and partial substitution of the external debt with domestic. Starting from 2003, Ministry of Finance began to prepare mid-term strategy for the development of the government bond market.

The average weighted effective yield for government bonds declined from 23.6 to 6.8 percent between end 2000 and the end of 2005. The effective yield for one-year bond declined from 21–22 percent by end 2000 to about 5 percent by end 2005 and turned negative in real terms starting in 2003. In 2003, the government extended the longest maturity from two to fifteen years in less than one year, although the 15-year issue was purchased and held primarily by Sberbank. In February 2006, the government began to place the 30 years OFZ. Overall, two-thirds of the demand for OFZs originates from state related institutions, including Sberbank and the Pension Fund of Russia that pursue a buy and hold strategy. As a result, liquidity on the secondary market is severely limited, with average market monthly turnover below 8 percent in the 2000–2005 periods. Also, market participants do not regard the OFZ yield curve as a market benchmark due to the high concentration of demand by state-related institutions, especially at the long end of the curve.

Following the 1998 Default, the Sub-Sovereign Bond Market Has Recovered Vigorously, with the Moscow Bond Emerging as the Benchmark for Both Sub-Sovereign and Corporate Bond Markets

The sub-sovereign bond market is growing rapidly. Sub-sovereign bond outstanding expanded from Rub23 billion by the end of 2001 to Rub161 billion by end-2005, or about US$5.6 billion. The number of issuers grew from 5 regions by end-2001 to 31 regions and 15 municipalities by the beginning of 2006. The number of exchange traded sub-national bond issues increased from 58 to about 100 over the same period.

Sub-sovereign yields have declined rapidly in the last four years. The Moscow (benchmark) annualized effective yield declined from 18 percent by the end of 2001 to around

5 percent by end-2005. Due to high liquidity, well developed yield curve, and investment grade credit rating (equal to the sovereign), the Moscow bond has become the benchmark for both sub-sovereign and corporate bond markets. In 2005, Moscow bonds traded at nearly sovereign level of yield. The spread of other sub-sovereign bonds has narrowed substantially as well, from up to 600 bps in 2002–03 to 250 bps by end-2005.

Secondary market liquidity has increased substantially with monthly turnover increasing from less than Rub10 billion by the end-2002 to Rub80 billion by end-2005. Liquidity is concentrated on Moscow and Moscow Oblast bonds as well as on St Petersburg bonds. The rest of the market is less liquid.

Commercial banks hold about 50–60 percent of sub-sovereign issues. Investment banks and asset management companies are the next largest investors. The share of non-state pension funds is small but growing rapidly, while the share of mutual funds and insurance companies remains marginal.

Since its Emergence in 2000, the Corporate Bond Market Has Grown Dynamically and Has Become Standardized Instrument for Debt Issuance by Medium and Large Corporations

Emerging in 2000 as a real financing option, the corporate bond market has grown dynamically. Bonds outstanding increased rapidly from Rub39 billion (about US$1.4 billion) by end 2000 to Rub481 billion by end 2005 (about US$16.7 billion). By the end of 2005, the market was comprised of over 310 bonds issued by about 220 issuers. About 80 percent of outstanding nominal amount do non-financial corporations issue bonds and around 20 percent are issued by financial institutions.

Until 2002, the market did not have any standards for bond terms, valuation methods and benchmarks. Issue sized remained small, ranging from Rub100 million to Rub3 billion. Only a few blue chips were traded while the rest of the bonds did not have a liquid secondary market. Official bond maturities ranged from one o three years, but since the market was not ready to absorb any paper with maturity greater than one year, most issuers offered binding buy-back options, which reduced the effective duration of the bonds to less than one year. In 2003–04, the corporate bond market became more standardized and mature. Issuers started place larger bonds of set sizes, with more fixed coupon rates and with fewer put options. Taking advantage of favorable market conditions in 2003, Gazprom placed a Rub10 billion issue with three years maturity without a put option. As of the end of 2005, the average weighted duration of corporate issues was about three years and average issue size grew to about Rub5 billion. For the last three years, the Moscow bond was the benchmark for the corporate bond market.

Secondary market liquidity has increased substantially with average monthly turnover for corporate bonds on MICEX growing from Rub0.5 billion in 2000 to about Rub75 billion in 2005. The secondary trading in corporate bonds has by far exceeded turnover of the government securities market. The market consists of three tiers. Tier I consists of the largest and most liquid issues by well-known corporations in the resources and infrastructure sectors, most of which as controlled or supported by the state. This segment accounts for about a third of the market. Most issues are rated by at least on global rating agency, and priced at 0 to 120 bps above the Moscow bond. Tier II consists of large and medium size issues of good credit quality of small/medium issues by the best credit quality Russian corporates. This market segment accounts for less then one third of the market. The majority of these issues are rated and priced at 120–300 bps above Moscow. Tier III consists of largely illiquid, small issues of reasonable or poor credit quality. These issues are not rated and their issuers mostly do not produce financial statements according to international standards. These issues are priced at 400 bps and above with respect to Moscow bonds.

The investor base for corporate bonds is dominated by banks. However, the role of institutional investors is growing steadily. The share of banks' holdings in corporate bonds declined from 70 percent in 2002 to less than 50 percent in 2005. At the same time, the share of institutional investors grew from 20 to 40 percent over the same period, with insurance firms and the non-state pension funds account for the largest portion of institutional investors holding. Starting in 2004, non-resident investors became quite active on the market, with their share increasing to over 10 percent in 2005.

Equity Market Capitalization Has Expanded Rapidly Over the Last Five Years, with Considerable Broadening and Deepening Since the Beginning of 2005 Despite Growing Competition from Offshore Equity Issuance and Trading

Equity market capitalization grew rapidly in the last five years from Rub1.2 trillion (US$41 billion or 15 percent of GDP) by end-2000 to about Rub15 trillion (over US$500 billion or about 70 percent of GDP) by end of 2005. The market capitalization growth in 2005 was most remarkable—in just one year the capitalization more than doubled from Rub6.9 trillion by end of 2004. Prior to 2005, capitalization expanded mostly due to price appreciation of Tier I and Tier II companies. Most of the capitalization growth in 2005 was still attributed to the price appreciation of blue chip issues, primarily Gazprom. At the same time, some increase in capitalization of 2005 was attributed to the new stocks admitted to trading, which grew from 215 at the end of 2004 to 277 at the end of 2005.

Despite rapid growth in capitalization, the market remains highly concentrated in terms of volume and trading activity among a dozen issuers, mostly in the oil and gas, electricity, metals and telecoms. In 2005, the top 10 blue chips accounted for 76 percent of market capitalization.

Prior to 2004, there were only two quasi-IPOs on the domestic equity market. Starting from 2004 Russian companies began to tap the domestic equity market, with seven IPOs placed on domestic exchanges in 2004–2005, and more issues in the pipeline for 2006. However, most Russian companies do not see the domestic market a major source of funds. Most issuers are ready to conduct domestic IPO only to comply with regulations and then raise funds through ADRs and GDRs on international markets. The equity issuance on international markets has increased substantially in 2005, with companies and major shareholders raising over US$4 billion through ADRs, GDRs, and foreign SPVs placed on international markets, primarily on London Stock Exchange, by comparison with US$223 million raised on MICEX and RTS.

Starting in 2003–04, secondary trading in Russian securities started to shift to international markets, causing major concern for domestic market institutions and the market regulator. As a result, the turnover of Russian depository receipts in LSE, Deutsche Borse and NYSE exceeded domestic trading on MICEX and RTS combined since the last quarter of 2003. This was reversed in 2005 when liquidity reverted back to the domestic market, with MICEX and RTS now accounting for 60 percent of Russian equity turnover by the end of the year, as a result of high ruble liquidity and dearth of available Russian instruments on international markets.

The Investment Fund Industry Has Expanded Significantly Over the Last Five Years, But is Dominated by Closed-end Funds Established by Corporations as an Investment and Tax Saving Vehicle

The investment fund industry took off following the adoption of the Investment Fund Law of 2001, which regulated two types of funds. Corporate investment funds (AIFs) established as corporations sell ordinary shares through open subscription only and are managed by an asset management company (AMC). Unit investment funds (PIFs) are established as a pool of assets under a trust management agreement between the investor and the trust management company (AMC). PIFs can operate as open-end funds (shares redeemable daily), close-end funds (shares redeemable at end of term of the trust agreement) and interval funds (shares redeemable at a term or interval set by the trust agreement).

The net asset value (NAV) of AIFs and PIFs grew from Rub8.8 billion by end-2000 to Rub230 billion by end-2005 or about 1.1 percent of GDP. The growth of the industry has been led by closed-end funds, most of which were established by Russian corporations as an investment and tax saving vehicle. By end 2005, the NAV of closed-end funds accounted for 70 percent of the value of all PIFs, compared to 17 percent for interval funds and 13 percent for open-end funds. Most open-end and interval funds are formed as equity, bonds, or balanced funds. Most closed-end funds are formed as equity, balanced, bond, or real estate funds. Venture capital and index funds are also gaining popularity. Money market funds are rare.

The number of licensed AMCs has grown rapidly over the 2003–05 period, partially due to the introduction of the pension reform, under which AMCs could obtain a license to manage Pillar II pension funds (See below). About two-thirds of AMCs had mutual funds under management in 2004, while the other asset managers specialized in pension funds only.

PIF investors have grown rapidly from 6 thousand at the end of 2000 to 122 thousand by end-2005 (in addition to 1.2 thousand investors of former voucher funds).

Non-state Pension Funds Have Grown Substantially Since Their Introduction in 1992, But Remain Dominated by Pension Funds Established by Corporations to Finance Own Investments

Since their introduction in 1995, the number of non-state pension funds (NSPFs) has grown to around 260 by end 2005. The pension reserves of the NSPF industry grew from mere Rub4 billion by end 1998 to about Rub200 billion (or about 1 percent of GDP) by end 2005.The sector is heterogeneous and concentrated, with the pension reserves of the 10 largest NSPFs above US$80 million and the reserves of about half of the NSPFs remaining below US$1 million. The largest NSPFs have been established and maintained by large corporations.

By end September 2005, NSPFs covered 5.9 million people, or about 8 percent of the economically active population. Most of these are covered indirectly through corporate funds, which account for more than 90 percent of the client base and 99 percent of contributions. Up to 2004, only about 600 thousand people joined pension funds independently due to high cost. At this stage, the ability of NSPFs to substantially raise pension replacement rates remains low (about 37 percent of average size of labor pension in mid 2004).

NSPFs investments are heavily dominated by equity, in particular stock of their parent company. This raises concerns about the financial security of the assets accumulated in NSPFs, and indicates that many NSPFs have been established with the objective to provide financing for large enterprises investments, rather than for providing an optimal, prudent combination of assets where individual pension savings could be invested to further protect them in old age.

The Insurance Sector Has Grown Steadily Over the Last Five Years, Although Until Recently Tax Avoidance Schemes Constituted a Significant Share of Voluntary Life and Property Insurance

The Russian insurance market has grown steadily over the past five years. Gross insurance premiums have grown from Rub171 billion in 2000 to Rub472 billion in 2004, and market penetration (Gross premiums/GDP) grew from 2.3 percent in 2000 to 2.8 percent by 2004. The structure of the market has changed slightly with the share of voluntary insurance declining from 82 to 76 percent and the share of compulsory insurance increasing from 18 to 24 percent of the total. With the adoption of the motor third party liability in July 2003, the share of compulsory insurance has increased substantially and expected to expand even more in the coming years.

Until 2003, significant share of voluntary life and property insurance constituted of tax avoidance schemes such as wage schemes. Under life insurance schemes, employers provide compensation for their workers and avoid the burden of social and other taxes on that compensation. Insurance contracts are surrendered within a short period following payment of the premium. This translates into aberrant claims to payments ratios ranging between 89 percent in 1999 to 131 percent in 2002. EU studies estimate that the size of the life insurance market outside wage schemes is about 11 percent of the market including wage schemes. Under property insurance schemes, companies use property insurance payments as additional losses to reduce tax claims. The introduction of new tax rules in 2003 and an industry-wide campaign by the All Russian Insurance Association have reportedly reduced the impact of wage schemes, and the largest companies are abandoning this gray market. While several small companies are still providing these services, effective implementation of the recently introduced minimum capital requirements should force them out of the market.

Insurance companies have rapidly diversified their investment portfolio away from government bonds toward higher yield investments, in particular corporate and sub-sovereign bonds (about 19 percent of total portfolio in mid-2005).

Until 2003, the geographical destination of reinsurance was heavily skewed toward the Baltic countries, which accounted for about two thirds of the total. The concentration of reinsurance to these markets as opposed to major established OECD reinsurance markets may be an indicator of the incidence of money laundering in the sector.

CHAPTER 2

Securities Markets: Key Impediments for Further Development and Policy Challenges Ahead

Legal and Regulatory Framework

The Legislative Framework for Securities Market Does Not Fully Cover Some Key Dimensions of the Securities Market, Such as Derivatives, Exchanges Trade Regulation, Insider Trading and Price Manipulation, Corporate Mergers, and Securitization

To bring the domestic market up to international standards and make it competitive in comparison with major international securities exchanges, a number of legal, regulatory, and infrastructure issues remain to be addressed. Required improvements include *inter alia* the introduction and enforcement of effective rules against insider trading and price manipulation; introduction of legal protection for derivatives transactions; and introduction of a centralized clearing and settlement system to streamline securities trading and reduce transaction cost and risk.

The existing legal framework for securities markets is fragmented and consists of many individual and often times inconsistent legislative acts. Over the medium-term, it would be advisable to restructure this framework into fewer but mutually consistent legislative acts, focusing laws on general regulatory principles and leaving detailed regulations for specific regulatory acts that can be amended more easily.

The FSFM is Working on Filling Key Gaps in the Legal and Regulatory Framework

Development of the Legal Base for Derivatives. The derivatives market is extremely limited due to the absence of a sound legal base. Under current legislation, the parties' rights and

7

obligations in derivatives transactions, as well as accounting and taxation of derivative transactions are not clearly defined. The Civil code currently treats derivatives transactions as "gambling transactions" (wagers), which are not subject to legal protection under the Code.

To address this issue, FSFM has prepared a draft Law on Derivatives and necessary amendments to the Civil Code, which needs to be adopted by the Government.

Development of Exchange Trade Regulation. Russian trading floors lag behind major international trading floors in terms of turnover, liquidity, and pricing efficiency. Russian exchanges still operate on expensive terms of pre-depositing and pre-funding, as opposed to full DVP with guaranteed execution settlement used on most major international exchanges. Due to these inefficiencies, a considerable part of Russian equities is traded abroad. In the absence of legal base and infrastructure, Russian investors hedge most of Russian securities risk through derivatives traded on international markets.

To address this issue, FSFM intends to develop a special Law "On Exchanges and Exchange Activities" which would streamline and improve the organization of trading for stocks, bonds, currencies, and commodities on futures. The law would clarify the legal structure of exchanges, set clear shareholder structure requirements and corporate governance system to make domestic exchanges more transparent and attractive for investors. The regulator also intends to transfer certain regulatory powers to exchanges in relation to traders and issuers.

Adoption of Law "On Inside Information and Market Regulation." Currently, there are no effective penalties for inside trading and price manipulation. Existing legislation does not define "insider" and "inside information." The law "On Securities Markets" contains a definition of "office information" and prohibits trading on it. However, the existing definition of inside information is inadequate and existing penalties limited. The same law also contains a definition of "price manipulation" and related penalties. However, the existing definition makes it difficult to prove a market participant guilty of such violation, and the possible penalty is limited only to suspension or canceling of professional licenses of market participants, which is not always adequate. Neither inside trading nor price manipulation involves criminal liability. As a result, these practices are common.

To address these problems, FSFM proposes to adopt a special law "On Inside Information and Market Manipulation" with related amendments in the law "On Securities Market," the RF Code on Administrative Violations and the RF Criminal Code. The already drafted law calls for administrative and criminal liability for the certain types of inside trading and price manipulation violations.

Regulation of Corporate Mergers. Current gaps in the corporate and securities market legislation are used by imprudent investors for gaining control over a target company at an unreasonably low price through various abuses of the law. Unfriendly and unfair corporate takeovers are becoming a common practice. These abuses undermine regular investors' trust in Russian stock market investments. At the moment, Article 80 of the Securities Market Law sets specific responsibilities for entities that intend to purchase 30 percent or more of voting shares in the joint-stock company. However, existing regulations are not sufficient.

To address these issues, FSFM intend to introduce additional amendments to the Securities Market Law and the Law on Joint-Stock Companies in order to introduce more effective regulation for corporate takeovers and the enforcement for related regulations. Clear and fair rules for corporate takeovers would raise investors' confidence in the stock market investment and would improve overall investment climate in Russia.

Adoption of Legislation on Securitization. Asset-backed securities do not exist in Russia due to the lack of the relevant securitization legislation. Under current Securities Market Law, a financial asset is recognized as a security only if there is a direct indication of this security in the law. The adoption of the Loan Mortgage Securities in 2004 is the first step accomplished by regulator and the government toward the development of asset-backed securities sector.

At the moment, FSFM is drafting a Law on Securitization. In addition, it would be necessary to amend the Civil Code, the Tax Code, the Law on Joint Stock Companies, the Law on Securities Markets, the Law on Insolvency (Bankruptcy), the Law on Foreign Currency Regulation, and the Law on Banks and Banking Activity. In particular, FSFM would need to obtain support and approval from CBR (banking regulator) since CBR would have to introduce the necessary amendments to the Law on Foreign Currency Regulation and the Law on Banks and Banking Activity.

Market Infrastructure

The Development of the Securities Market is Hampered by Deficiencies in Market Infrastructure

The development of the securities market is hampered by deficiencies in market infrastructure, including: (i) high degree of market fragmentation, with several markets competing with each other and offering their own settlement and clearing procedures; (ii) high risk related to record keeping of the holder of registered securities (registrar risk); (iii) low adaptability of record keeping system to foreign registration and settlement systems; (iv) high cost of pre-deposit funds and pre-funding and high risk on non-payment under free delivery method; (vi) absence of RTGS and (vii) low transparency of OTC market.

The merger of the two CSDs into a Central Depository (CD) and centralized clearing would eventually allow Russian exchanges to trade on the basis of the delivery vs. payment system (DVP) in line with international standards. However, since this concentrates risks, the authorities will need to adopt international standards for risk control (CPSS/IOSCO among others) and to develop oversight capacity to ensure that these standards are met.

Over time, the registrar industry will need to be rationalized. In the short term, requirements for registrars that serve publicly traded companies could be tightened. The CSD could establish a common IT system to serve the registrar industry. Over time, the CSD would become the mandatory registrar for publicly traded companies.

The post-trade transparency of RTS and MICEX are of a reasonable standard to meet the needs of the market. However, the transparency of OTC trading is extremely low and not in line with international standards. Reporting of OTC trades to RTS is voluntary. Reporting to the regulator takes place as part of periodical financial reporting and only for administrative purposes. A substantial share of OTC trades is reported to settlement depositaries, but these data are not readily available to the public.

Reporting of OTC trades should be mandatory. End-of-day reporting could be established for a start, and reporting rule subsequently tightened in line with international standards. The regulator should establish procedures to ensure that traders effectively comply with these rules.

FSFM is Focusing on Key Measures to Address the Most Important Deficiencies in Market Infrastructure

Going forward, FSFM is addressing the most important deficiencies in market infrastructure focusing on:

- establishing the CSD system, amending the Law on Clearing to introduce centralized settlement and clearing, and capitalizing the system;
- ensuring that effective RTGS system is in place, at least on MICEX and RTS; enabling DVP settlement to replace pre-deposit fund and securities system;
- improving registrars system through consolidation of existing registrars, evaluating the linkages between CSD and registrars, and evaluating the CSD as registrar for listed securities; and
- Adopting international standards for risk control (CPSS/IOSCO among others) and developing oversight capacity to ensure that these standards are met.

Government Bonds

Following Years of Limited Federal Bond Market Activity, a Number of Recent Developments Point to a Potential Revitalization of the Market

Following years of limited market activity, reflecting in large part improved Federal budget position and improved sovereign rating, a number of recent development point to a potential revival of the domestic government bond market. In 2004, the Government adopted a debt strategy to increase reliance on domestic debt and limit foreign currency issuance. At the same time, the authorities increased their reliance on marketable securities on the domestic market, lengthened the average maturity profile of the debt portfolio, and proposed the introduction of benchmark issues, while CBR discontinued its purchases of government bonds in the primary market. The authorities also proposed the introduction of a primary dealer system. Starting from January 1, 2007, all restrictions on foreign investors investment into government bonds will be lifted.

However, Despite These Developments, Numerous Impediments to Market Development Remain

The Government Debt Market is Highly Fragmented. The Federal domestic debt portfolio remains fragmented, with a large number of different types of instruments and a large number of individual issues outstanding within each instrument category. This contrasts with most OECD countries where government debt is increasingly composed of small number of more liquid benchmark bonds and where refinancing risk is managed through market-based reverse auctions and switching programs.

A Large Portion of Outstanding Government Debt is Concentrated in Buy and Hold Portfolios. CBR, Sberbank, the Pension Fund of Russia (PFR) and the State Asset Management Company (GUK) account for a majority of government bond holdings, and hold these securities under buy and hold strategies. With the exception of PFR, non-bank financial institutions participation in the market remains marginal, reflecting the limited yield/liquidity attractiveness of government paper and limited development of institutional savings sector.

The Primary Issuance Process Lacks Transparency. The government securities market lacks a transparent and predictable issuance process based on well-documented auction calendars and issuance plans. While some progress has been made, the time period and detail covered in MOF's announcements falls short of investors' requirements and is not in line with practices in OECD countries.

There is No Primary Dealer System. Market development is hampered by the absence of a primary dealer (PD) system. While this system will not in itself resolve all the structural problems facing the market, experience in OECD countries has shown that an effective primary dealership framework can contribute significantly to market depth and liquidity.

There is Absence of Full Open Market Pricing of Primary Market Yields. The dominant position of Sberbank on the market, combined with low issuance and high demand for government securities by banks to manage liquidity needs has resulted in emergence of partially captive market with yields below what would otherwise prevail, curtailing investment demand by discretionary (i.e. non-captive) investors. As a result, in a full open market environment, secondary yields would tend to be higher than primary yields, giving rise to capital losses.

Secondary Market Activity is Very Limited, and Government Bonds Do Not Constitute the Benchmark for the Domestic Bond Market. As a result of the above factors and of deficiencies in market infrastructure, the government securities market is illiquid. As a result of limited liquidity and concentrated investor base, government bonds do not constitute the benchmark for the domestic bond market. This role is played by the City of Moscow bonds.

To Address These Impediments, the Authorities Can Take a Number of Key Measures.

First, to Prepare Medium-term Federal Debt Strategy. Preparation of medium-term Federal debt strategy would include objective, funding plans, plans for consolidation of issues, reverse auctions and switching, concentration of issuance and benchmarks, auction calendar, and arrangements for primary auction process.

Second, to Increase the Transparency of the Auction System. The authorities can take a number of measures to increase the transparency of the auction system, in particular:

- embodying auctions procedures in a standing MOF regulation,
- announcing auction calendars well in advance,

- holding multiple auctions on the same date,
- allowing the market to set the cut-off rate,
- limiting Sberbank dominant market position through limiting bid size from a single bidder,
- establishing maximum amount for non-competitive bids and a minimum amount for competitive bids. Establishing an overall limit on the amount of non-competitive bids,
- broaden eligibility for participation in auction to non-banks, although the latter may be required to bid through or with the guarantee of a bank, and
- limiting after auction sale of additional securities by MOF.

Third, to Implement Primary Dealer System. The authorities can consider setting-up a market-making mechanism through a primary dealer system. A realistic balance would need to be achieved between the responsibilities and privileges of PDs in order to ensure that they provide liquidity to the market and that the system is commercially viable. This would require clear regulations re selection, monitoring and retention of individual PDs, as well as pre and post-auction price analysis to guard against collusion.

Sub-Sovereign Bonds

In Recent Years, Authorities Have Taken a Broad Range of Measures to Strengthen the Legal and Regulatory Framework for Sub-Sovereign Borrowing

First, Development and Implementation of Prudential Framework for Sub-sovereign Borrowing. The authorities have developed and implemented a comprehensive prudential framework for sub-sovereign borrowing, including debt outstanding limit, budget deficit limit, current expenditure limit, debt service limit, and guarantee limit. In addition, foreign borrowing is limited to refinancing of existing foreign debt by Subjects of the Federation (SFs), and municipalities are prohibited to borrow in foreign currency. This framework provides a sound basis for market access by sub-sovereign entities. In particular, the current expenditure limit ensures that borrowing is for investment purposes only.

Second, Procedures in Case of Breach of Prudential Regulations or Debt Default. The authorities have introduced provisions allowing higher levels of the Federal system to intervene and take control of budget execution of lower levels in case of breach of prudential regulations or in case of debt default by a sub-sovereign entity.

Third, Regulations for Sub-sovereign Bond Registration and Listing. The authorities have adopted detailed procedures for the registration of sub-sovereign securities by the Ministry of Finance and for their listing on the stock exchange (MICEX). These procedures allow MOF to ensure that entities issuing securities on the market respect rules and regulations concerning budget execution and prudential limits, and appropriate disclosure to investors.

Despite These Considerable Advances, Several Deficiencies Remain in the Legal and Regulatory Framework for Sub-Sovereign Borrowing

First, some of the regions that broke one or two prudential limits set by budget code were still allowed to issue bonds.

Second, sub-sovereign entities are in some cases shareholders of regional banks that make loans to them, often on favorable terms, significantly raising moral hazard.

Third, the framework for intervention by higher levels of the Federal system in case of debt default remains vague. In particular, the Budget Code does not regulate the procedural issues of transfer of budget management responsibility to a different level of the Federal system in case of default.

The Government Can Take a Number of Key Measures to Address These Deficiencies

The authorities can focus on a number of key measures to support the development of the domestic sub-sovereign bond market:

- Enforce prudential limits by denying approvals for bond issuance for SFs and municipalities in breach of these limits.
- Include past due payments in calculation of indebtedness limits.
- Eliminate new related party borrowing from affiliated banks, and enforce standards for competitive selection for bank creditors and bond underwriters.
- Adopt law on bankruptcy of regions and municipalities, substituting for current provisions on sub-sovereign debt default in the Budget Code.

Corporate Bonds

Corporate Bond Market Risk is Increasing

The overheating of the corporate bond market poses a growing market risk arising from the increasing disconnect between corporate bond yields and the riskiness of specific issues, and from the possible 9impact of a corporate bond default on the risk perception of investors.

The Authorities are Taking Several Measures to Reduce Market Risk Through Improving Disclosure by Corporations Listed on Exchanges

The authorities are taking a number of measures to improve the extent and quality of disclosure by corporations listed on exchanges:

- Encouraging listed corporations to improve their accounting standards through the adoption of IAS,
- Improving the governance of listed corporations through the adoption of the Corporate Governance Code, and
- Establishing differential corporate governance requirements in MICEX and RTS listing categories, on the basis of self-declaration.

Going forward, the authorities could focus on the following actions:

■ Adopt a realistic calendar for the adoption of new listing rules including IAS requirement for listing on MICEX and RTS (first tier),
■ Require listed companies to disclose their ultimate economic beneficiaries, and
■ Adopt specific Governance Code criteria and enforce their implementation by listed companies.

Equities

The Development of the Equity Market is Subject to a Number of Supply Side and Demand Side Constraints

On the supply side, the heavy concentration of the market in a few large companies may be an impediment for market development, as large companies tend to place their IPOs abroad and as medium-size companies may feel too small to access the domestic market on their own or may be reluctant to access the market for fear of takeover. For those companies that are listed on the market, free float remains low (from 5 to 25 percent).

On the demand side, broad participation by domestic investors is impeded by the absence of effective legal base for prevention of price manipulation and unfair market practices. Absence of Law on Insider Trading, lack of requirement for reporting under IAS and lack of independent verification and monitoring of adherence to corporate governance code criteria may act as further deterrent to investor participation.

The rapid increase in the share of Russian equity turnover on foreign exchanges, primarily LSE, results from inefficient infrastructure and high transactions costs (high transaction risk, ownership registration) on domestic exchanges.

The Authorities Can Take a Number of Key Actions to Address These Constraints

The authorities can take a number of key actions to address the impediments to equity market development, namely:

■ Adopt legislation on insider trading and price manipulation.
■ Improve regulation of hostile takeover.
■ Establish CD, introduce centralized settlement and clearing system.
■ Allow foreign securities trading though RDRs on MICEX and RTS.
■ Adopt calendar for IAS reporting for listed companies.
■ Enforce Governance Code criteria for listed companies.

CHAPTER 3

Institutional Investors: Key Impediments for Further Development and Policy Challenges Ahead

Mutual Funds

*The Adoption of the Investment Funds Law in 2001 Has Established
a Firm Legal Base for the Development of the Industry*

The law clarified many established practices in the industry, such as mandatory disclosure rules on price, registration of prospectuses, licensing of managers, and minimum capital requirements. It also introduced new provisions allowing trading of funds on secondary market and the formation of closed-end funds. Regulations adopted by FSFM have further clarified operational procedures for the industry, and the tax regime of unit investment funds (PIFs) was clarified by related instructions from MOF. FSFM plays a particularly important role in protecting investor's rights in open-end and interval funds.

*Despite This Progress, Several Deficiencies Hamper the Development
of the Investment Fund Industry*

A number of deficiencies hamper the development of the investment fund industry.

FSFM can impose sanctions against a joint stock fund, management company, depository or other licensed authority only under the Administrative Code. However, fines under the Code are insufficient. FSFM has the authority to suspend distribution of shares over a six-month period. However, FSFN does not have authority to revoke the license of a registered management company or investment trust.

The Investment Funds Law does not contain any provisions, which would hold natural persons working for a legal entity liable for violations of the Law.

FSFM does not have sufficient investigation authority to properly monitor the industry. While it has access to fund books and records, FFSM cannot question third parties that are often critical to any securities investigations. However, FSFM has the power to go to court on behalf of investors if the Law has been broken by a licensed entity.

Although the Law prohibits a depository, registrar, auditor or appraiser of the assets of the joint-stock investment fund from also being a shareholder in the fund, it does not prohibit a third entity, such as a financial conglomerate, from being a controlling shareholder in both entities. The same also applies to employees of the above entities and of financial conglomerates.

The Authorities Can Take a Number of Measures to Address These Deficiencies

The authorities can take a number of measures to address these deficiencies:

- ▩ Strengthen enforcement powers of FSFM over investment funds and fund management companies, including authority to annul licenses and authority to apply fines.
- ▩ Strengthen investigative powers of FSFM over funds, fund management companies and registrars.
- ▩ Establish provisions holding natural persons liable for violations of the Law, acting individually or on behalf of a legal entity (fund, fund management company).
- ▩ Strengthen independence between financial conglomerates and their employers and joint stock investment funds, unit investment funds, fund depositories, registrars and auditors.
- ▩ Specify disclosure requirements for fund management companies (possible already specified).

Pension Funds

The Development of the Private Pension Fund Market Faces Three Major Impediments

Deficiencies in the Regulatory and Supervisory Framework for Funded Pensions. Non-State Pension funds (NSPFs) are insufficiently regulated and supervised. A large number of NSPFs are company plans run by large employers as source of financing for company shares and investments, rather than as mechanism to optimize returns for beneficiaries while minimizing risks. Market-based pension funds are limited in number. As a result, the trust of savers in these funds is low and could be easily lost. The transfer of supervision authority for pension funds to FSFM provides an opportunity to strengthen the regulatory and supervisory framework for the industry.

Lack of Protection of Contributors' Rights. The legal and regulatory framework does not adequately protect contributor's rights. These pertain to non-discrimination in access, vested rights and rights of pension fixed irrespective of contributors, and portability. In particular, vested rights are only regulated on an ad-hoc and case-by-case basis, leaving them to arbitrary management.

Lack of Public Awareness and Information Disclosure. Despite the increase in the number of clients in the NSPF sector, the vast majority of the population are not aware of NSPF activities and private retirement benefit schemes, and the minority who are aware of these schemes are suspicious. NSPFs are required to provide large amounts of information to the regulator, but this information is not disclosed to the public, creating an information gap that is filled by mistrust in NSPFs.

The Authorities can Act to Address These Impediments Through a Number of Specific Actions

Key actions include:

- Strengthen regulation and supervision of NSPFs in accordance with international standards.
- Strictly limit the share of NSPF portfolio that can be invested in the NSPF founding company.
- Establish and enforce comprehensive disclosure rules for NSPFs.

Insurance Companies

The Development of the Insurance Sector Faces a Number of Major Impediments

Lack of Separation between Life and Non-Life Insurance. Following the adoption of the new Law on Insurance in 2004, the effective separation between life and non-life insurance will be achieved only in 2007. From the time of adoption of the new Law, however, insurance companies were prohibited to stop writing either of the two businesses and to notify the supervisory body of their choice. Effective separation of life and non-life insurance companies will require comprehensive re-licensing of existing insurance companies in 2007.

Undercapitalization of Insurance Companies. Following the adoption of the new Law on Insurance in 2004, insurance companies need to meet higher capital requirements. Given that a vast majority of insurance companies are undercapitalized, this requirement will lead to a substantial reduction in the number of companies, leaving about 400–500 companies on the market compared to about 1400 at the beginning of 2004. There are concerns that several small companies may falsify their records to justify compliance. The Federal Insurance Supervision Service (FISS) therefore faces a major challenge in enforcing the higher capital requirement established under the Law.

Limited Capacity to Carry Out Actuarial Assessment of Reserves. Under the new Law, insurance companies are required to carry out an actuarial assessment of reserves and file an actuarial report with their annual financial statements starting July 1, 2007. The limited availability of actuaries poses a major challenge for the insurance industry in meeting this requirement.

Difficulties in Implementing Compulsory Motor Third Party Liability Insurance (MTPL). The implementation of MTPL introduced in 2002 faces a number of difficulties. First, insurance companies need to develop their capacity to ensure sound and proper claims handling practices. Second, claims reserves need to be properly kept and accounted for. Third, there is a need to establish a proper system to combat fraud. Fourth, the current requirement of intervention of police officer even when no personal injury is involved in highly ineffective and amicable settlement forms will need to be introduced.

Limitations to Foreign Participation in the Sector. Starting in 2004, the maximum total quota of foreign capital allowed in the Russian market was raised from 15 to 25 percent. All limitations have been waived for insurance companies participated or fully owned by foreign investors belonging to EU member states. All other foreign insurers and investors are still subjected to the above limitations. In addition, cross border direct insurance and branching are prohibited.

Absence of Consumer Protection Rules. Consumer confidence is undermined by the lack of consumer protection rules in the sector. These rules should operate at two levels. First, at the contractual level, by means of new legal rules aimed at monitoring unfair terms in consumer contracts, providing guidance for the interpretation of standard forms, establishing non-waivable consumer rights of cancellation, withdrawal, and information. Second, at the enforcement level, by means of new legal rules aimed at governing claims handling practices and introducing alternative dispute resolution mechanisms.

Weaknesses in the Legal and Regulatory Framework. The new FISS is not financially independent from the Ministry of Finance and has insufficient human and technical resources to effectively perform its supervisory tasks.

The FISS does not have power to apply fit and proper tests for controllers and significant owners of insurance companies, contrary to IAIS requirements Moreover, the FISS is not entrusted with the power to approve/refuse the acquisition and/or transfer of qualifying holdings in insurance undertakings (changes in control), nor to check the source of funds to acquire control in an insurance company.

The FISS does not have the power to take resolution measures against companies that do not adhere to the law and to regulations, such as to impose obligations to take adequate measures and remove the violation, to require convening of extraordinary shareholders meeting; to impose fines for non-compliance, to dismiss the management and appoint provisional administration; and to adopt financial recovery plan to reestablish financial stability of an insurance undertaking. In addition, FISS does not have a degree of immunity and legal protection for all actions taken in good faith and without negligence.

There are currently no specific rules on supplemental supervision for insurance companies belonging to an insurance group or to a financial conglomerate. It is particularly important to examine problems related to double gearing, capital leverage, and intra-group transactions that may have a negative impact on the solvency situation of insurance undertakings. This requires enhanced collaboration between FISS and other Federal supervisory agencies in the supervision of financial conglomerates.

Current reinsurance activities also require special attention, given the high share of reinsurance outside well-established reinsurance markets. The FISS lacks express powers to monitor and review insurance programs of supervised entities, to assess the quality of domestic and foreign reinsures, and to mandate changes when required. This also requires enhanced collaboration with foreign supervisory authorities on cross-border insurance and reinsurance activities with the objective of preventing money laundering and other illegal activities.

Finally, current regulations and supervision of investment activities of insurance companies needs to be strengthened. Insurers need to comply with standards on investment activities, including requirements on investment policy, asset mix, valuation, diversification, asset-liability management, and risk management.

Lack of Internal Control (Audit) Function. Currently, insurance companies lack an internal control/audit function. This function is needed to provide a systematic and disciplined approach to evaluating and improving the effectiveness of the operation and ensuring compliance with laws and regulations.

The Authorities Can Take a Number of Measures to Address These Impediments.

Key priorities are:

- Establish FISS as an independent agency with its own funding sources.
- Strengthen coordination between FISS, MOF and other Federal regulatory agencies.
- Strictly enforce minimum capital requirements.
- Grant FISS the power to check fitness and propriety of qualified shareholders, controllers and beneficial owners of insurance companies at licensing/re-licensing stage, and to approve subsequent changes in control of supervised entities.
- Strengthen monitoring by FISS of investment activities and changes in investment portfolio of insurance undertakings.
- Establish clear anti-money laundering procedures.
- Establish rules on supplemental supervision of insurance companies belonging to insurance groups or financial conglomerates.
- Require insurance companies to have an internal audit function.
- Enact consumer protection rules.

TECHNICAL ANNEXES

Recent Macroeconomic and Financial Sector Developments

Macroeconomic Environment

In the early years of transition, macroeconomic instability hampered the development of the financial sector in Russia. From three digits hyperinflation in 1993–95, inflation was brought below 50 percent in 1996, but increased sharply after the 1998 financial crisis to about 85 percent in 1999. Only in 2000 did the Government manage to bring inflation down to about 20 percent. Government deficits were financed through short-term securities (GKOs) held by banks for speculation and liquidity management. The August 1998 banking crisis was the result of the Government default on GKOs, combined with an economic slowdown caused by a sharp drop in commodity prices and a sharp devaluation of the ruble.

Russia successfully stabilized its economy after the financial crisis in 1998. GDP real growth since has averaged more than 6 percent and industrial output by more than 5 percent in the last five years. Moreover, inflation was brought down to a moderate range of 11–12 percent in 2003–05, while real exchange rate volatility was reduced. Russian government was running a growing budget surplus in the last five years, peaking at 7.5 percent in 2005. The Stabilization Fund, established by Russian government to accumulate additional revenues from high oil prices, totaled Rub522.3 billion (about US$18.7 billion) by end 2004, and reached Rub1,460 billion (about US$50.7 billion) by end 2005. Exports grew to the highest level since 1994 with Russia's current account and trade surplus reaching an all time high level of US$86.6 billion and US$120.2 billion respectively in 2005 (See Table 1 below). Rapid GDP growth, surplus oil revenues, and ruble appreciation against the U.S. dollar enabled the Russian Federation to reduce its external debt/GDP ratio from over 100 percent in 1999 to less than 12 percent by end 2005. As a result of macroeconomic and structural improvements the credit rating of Russian Federation by S&P global scale in foreign currency has been increased from CCC+ at the beginning of 2000 to BBB at the end of 2005.

The strong economic performance of the Russian economy in recent years is attributed mostly to the performance of the oil and gas sector. With oil and gas prices reaching all time highs, this sector has accounted for most of the GDP and export growth in recent years. Yet, to achieve sustainable growth over the medium to long-term, the Russian economy needs to increase productivity and value added in the other sectors of the economy. The dominance of the oil and gas sector poses a major threat to balanced economic development.

The financing of the resource-intensive sectors does not constitute a problem at the moment, since these export-oriented sectors are highly profitable and can generate ample cash flows in foreign currency as well as borrow funds on international markets. In the non-resource-intensive sector, retained earnings constitute over 70 percent of investment financing, while the domestic financial sector does not provide efficient intermediation. The funds generated by the resource sector are mostly spent within itself and there is not much spillovers to other sectors. Financing of other sectors remains weak. The level of financial intermediation in banking and financial system remains low compared to OECD economies but comparable to transitional economies. Moreover, the recent appreciation of the Ruble is making non-energy, non-metal subsectors non-competitive (Dutch disease).

Table 1: Key Macroeconomic Indicators

Exchange Rates	2000	2001	2002	2003	2004	2005
USD official rate, end of period	28.16	30.14	31.78	29.45	27.75	28.81
USD official rate, avg	28.13	29.17	31.35	30.69	28.81	28.28
Real effective exchange rates, 2000 = 100	100	118.72	122.66	126.99	136.52	

Output Indicators	2000	2001	2002	2003	2004	2005
GDP, Nominal R bn		7306	8944	10818	13243	17008	21665
GDP, Nominal USD bn		259.7	306.6	345.1	431.5	581.4	733.2
Real GDP Growth, % y-o-y		10.0	5.1	4.7	7.3	7.2	6.4
Industrial production, % change, y-o-y		11.9	4.9	3.7	7.0	8.3	4.0
Fixed capital investment, % change, y-o-y		17.4	8.7	2.6	12.5	10.9	10.5

Prices	2000	2001	2002	2003	2004	2005
Inflation (CPI), % change, p-o-p	20.2	18.6	15.1	12.0	11.7	10.9
PPI, % change, Y-o-Y	31.6	10.7	17.1	13.1	28.3	

Fiscal and Monetary Indicators	2000	2001	2002	2003	2004	2005
M2/GDP	21.5%	23.9%	26.4%	29.9%	31.2%	27.9%
M2, % change, p-o-p	58.8	44.6	34.1	44.8	42.5	
CBR Reserves (including gold) billion $, end-o-p	27.97	36.62	47.79	76.94	124.5	182.24

Table 1: Key Macroeconomic Indicators (Continued)

Exchange Rates	2000	2001	2002	2003	2004	2005
Stabilization Fund, R billion					522.3	1460.0
Stabilization Fund, $ billion					18.7	50.7

Federal Budget	2000	2001	2002	2003	2004	2005
Revenues, Cumulative (% of GDP)	15.5	17.8	20.4	19.6	20.4	35.1
Expenditures, Cumulative (% of GDP)	13.1	14.8	19	17.9	16.1	27.4
Consolidated Balance, % GDP	2.3	3	2.3	1.7	4.2	7.7
Primary balance, % of GDP	4.7	5.5	4.4	3.4	5.4	8.5

Balance of Payment Indicators	2000	2001	2002	2003	2004	2005
Trade Balance, $ billion	60.7	48.1	46.3	59.9	86.90	120.2
Current Account, $ billion	46.3	35.1	32.8	35.9	60.109	86.6
Exports, $ billion	105.6	101.9	107.3	135.9	183.2	
Imports, $ billion	44.9	53.8	61.0	76.1	96.3	
Average export price of Russia's oil, $/bbl	24.0	20.9	21.0	23.9	34.1	

Financial Market Indicators	2000	2001	2002	2003	2004	2005
Average deposit rate for enterprises, %	8.7	8.5	6.9	4.4	4.2	
Average lending rate for enterprises, %	24.3	17.9	15.8	13.1	11.5	
CBR refinancing rate, %, end-o-p	25.0	25.0	21.0	16.0	13.0	12.0
Real average rate for Ruble loans, % (deflated by PPI)	−15.8	−1.1	3.9	−2.2	−10.1	
Net credits to real sector, R billion	−15.0	486	479.0	897.8	1210.2	
Share of long-term credits to entrepr. in total, %	25.3	21.3	25.32	30	30	
Stock market index (RTS, ruble term)	142.4	260.1	359.1	567.3	614.1	1125.6

Enterprises Finances	2000	2001	2002	2003	2004	2005
Share of loss-making companies 1/	41.6	38.4	43.4	41.3	35.8	
Profitability (net profit/paid sales), % 1/	32.7	25.6	17.4	20.7	25.5	
Non-cash settlements (% of total sales)	30.7	22.3	18.03129	14.18	11.1	
Stock of overdue payables (% of sales), end-o-p		35.59	27.6	20.2	13.7	

Income, Poverty and Labor Market	2000	2001	2002	2003	2004	2005
Net change in gov't wage arrears, %, p-o-p	−51.4	−26.5	−5.2	−34.4	−55.5	−80.3
Real disposable income, 99 = 100	112.0	121.7	135.3	155.4	170.7966	185.8
Average dollar wage, US $	80.2	112.4	138.6	179.4	237	301.6
Share of people living below subsistence, % 1/	28.9	27.3	24.2	20.6	17.8	15.8
Unemployment (%, ILO definition)	10.5	9.0	8.1	8.6	8.2	7.6

1/ Cumulative from the year beginning.
Source: Goskomstat, CBR, EEG, IMF, staff estimates.

Figure 1. M2/GDP Dynamics

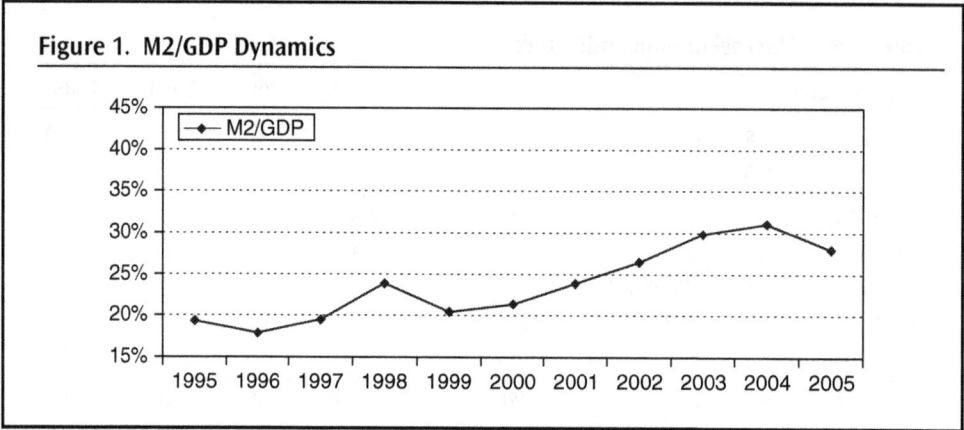

Source: CBR, Federal Statistics Service.

The monetization of the Russian economy grew at a rapid pace since the 1998 crisis (see Figure 1) reflecting both supply and demand factors. The current account surplus provided ample liquidity as the Central Bank has absorbed some of the foreign currency in exchange for local currency. CBR reserves grew from US$28 billion by end 2000 to US$182 billion by end 2005. Although financial intermediation strengthened significantly in the last five years, the growth in M2/GDP ratio was attributed more for the growing demand for real money balances by the private sector rather than more efficient financial intermediation.

Figure 2. Eurobonds Spreads to UST, bp

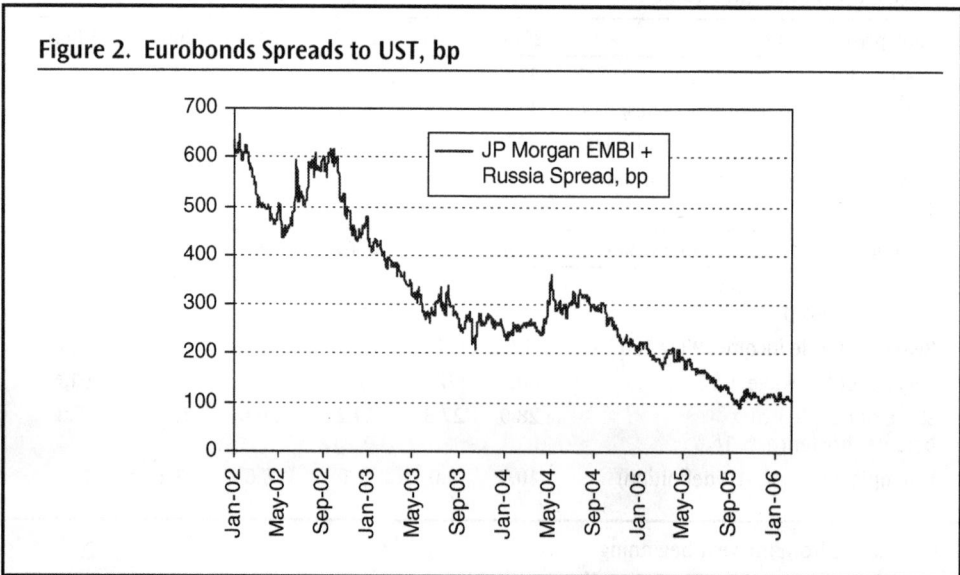

Source: JP Morgan (EMBI+ Russia Index).

Figure 3. OFZ Effective Yield, percent

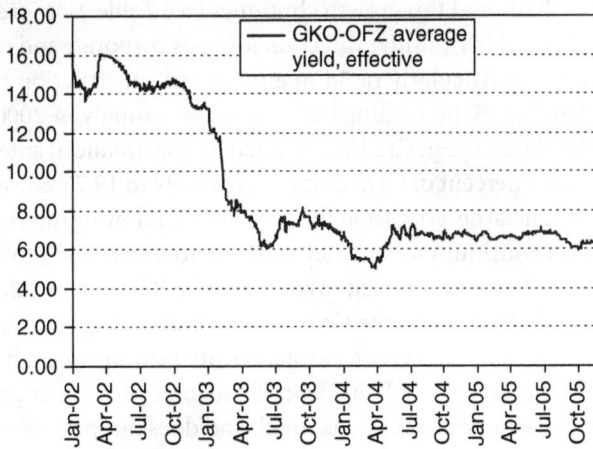

Source: Bank Zenit (Government bonds index).

As shown in Figure 2, the Government Eurobond interest rates of all maturities have declined over the last few years, mostly reflecting declining sovereign spreads as a result of improve sovereign credit rating. The decline in domestic interest rates has been more significant, and the GKO/OFZ (Russian government domestic bills and bonds) real yields have become negative since 2002 (see Figure 3).

Figure 4. Official Rub/US$ Exchange Rate 2001–06

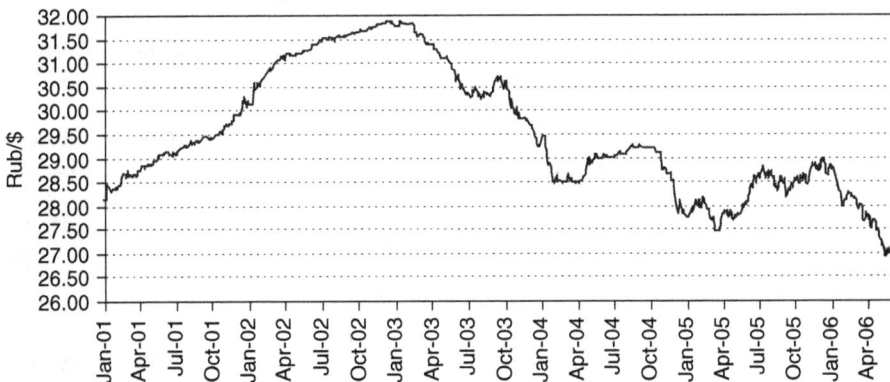

Source: CBR.

Banking Sector

Banking assets as a share of GDP grew rapidly from a low 24 percent by end of 1995 to 45 percent by end of 2005, and this growth continues (see Table 2). Moreover, the distribution of assets has changed in a positive direction towards corporate and retail sector credit. Credit growth has been particularly rapid in energy and construction related sectors, as well as consumer lending. Bank lending began to grow strongly in 2000, lagging behind enterprise growth by about a year. Credits extended to non-financial enterprises and organizations grew from 9.9 percent of GDP at the end of 1999 to 19.7 percent by end of 2004. Still, credit to non-financial enterprises at this level remains low by international standards and access to finance continues to be a key obstacle to enterprise growth. Bank credits financed only about 4.8 percent of fixed investments in 2003. The banks holding of government bonds and other claims on the Government is declining relative to GDP, and the same is true for foreign assets and credits to state owned enterprises. The volume of bank loans grew rapidly in the last 5 years. Bank deposit and loan rates for corporations declined. Overall, the size of banking sector remains small, and does not provide effective intermediation for the growing Russian economy.

Table 2: Banking Statistics

Quantitative Characteristics of Credit Institutions	2000	2001	2002	2003	2004	2005
Operating credit institutions licensed to conduct banking activities	1311	1319	1329	1329	1299	1253
o/w banks	1274	1276	1282	1277	1249	1205
o/w non-bank credit institutions	37	43	47	52	50	48

Macroeconomic Indicators of Banking Sector	2000	2001	2002	2003	2004	2005
Banking sector assets (liabilities), Rub bil.	2362.5	3159.7	4145.3	5600.7	7136.9	9750.3
as % of GDP	32.3%	35.3%	38.3%	42.3%	42.0%	45.0%
Banking sector equity capital, Rub bil.	286.4	453.9	581.3	814.9	946.6	1241.8
as % of GDP	3.9%	5.1%	5.4%	6.2%	5.6%	5.7%
as % of banking sector assets	12.1%	14.4%	14.0%	14.6%	13.3%	12.7%
Loans and other funds extended to resident non-financial enterprises including overdue debt, Rub bil.	802.7	1228.9	1654	2385	3268.7	4274.7
as % of GDP	11.0%	13.7%	15.3%	18.0%	19.2%	19.7%
as % of banking sector assets	34.0%	38.9%	39.9%	42.6%	45.8%	43.8%

Table 2: Banking Statistics (Continued)

Macroeconomic Indicators of Banking Sector	2000	2001	2002	2003	2004	2005
Loans extended to individuals including overdue debt, Rub bil.	44.7	94.7	142.2	299.7	618.9	1179.3
as % of GDP	5.6%	7.7%	8.6%	12.6%	18.9%	27.6%
as % of banking sector assets	1.9%	3.0%	3.4%	5.4%	8.7%	12.1%
Bank loans used for capital investment by companies, Rub bil.	29.5	48.7	65.1	94	156.5	
as % all capital investments by companies	2.9%	3.5%	4.8%	5.3%	7.3%	
Securities hold by banks, Rub bil.	473.2	562	779.9	1002.2	1086.9	1539.4
as % of GDP	6.5%	6.3%	7.2%	7.6%	6.4%	7.1%
as % of banking sector assets	20.0%	17.8%	18.8%	17.9%	15.2%	15.8%
Household deposits and other funds, Rub bil.	445.7	678.0	1029.7	1517.8	1977.2	2754.6
as % of GDP	6.1%	7.6%	9.5%	11.5%	11.6%	12.7%
as % of banking sector liabilities	18.9%	21.5%	24.8%	27.1%	27.7%	28.3%
Funds attracted from enterprises and organizations*	722.1	902.6	1091.4	1384.8	1986.1	2953.1
as % of GDP	9.9%	10.1%	10.1%	10.5%	11.7%	13.6%
as % of banking sector liabilities	30.6%	28.6%	26.3%	24.7%	27.8%	30.3%

Interest Rates	2000	2001	2002	2003	2004	2005
Average (year) deposit rate for enterprises, %	8.7	8.5	6.9	4.4	4.2	3.1
Average (year) lending rate for enterprises, %	24.3	17.9	15.8	13.1	11.5	10.9
CBR refinancing rate, %, end-o-p	25.0	25.0	21.0	16.0	13.0	12.0

* including deposits, government extra-budgetary funds, funds of the Ministry of Finance, financial bodies, customers in factoring and forfeiting operations, float, and funds written down from client's accounts but not entered in a credit institution's correspondent account.
Source: CBR.

Paradoxically, the Russian banking scene can be described to be both over-banked and under-served at the same time. The banking sector is highly concentrated in Moscow, St. Petersburg and other major urban centers. As of end of 2004, about half of the 1249 active banks and over 80 percent of the banking assets were concentrated in Moscow.

Furthermore, nearly 80 percent of private sector enterprises' deposits and over 60 percent of government deposits were placed in Moscow based banks, and enterprises located in Moscow received about half of the total bank loans to corporate sector.

Despite positive trends in the economy, the banking sector remains vulnerable. With one dominant state-owned bank (Sberbank), a handful of medium—to large sized money center banks and a plethora of small pocket banks, the structure of the sector is unbalanced reducing both the resilience of the system and its ability to serve the needs of the economy. Many banks likely overstate capital or have fictitious capital, and the CBR has difficulty in enforcing capital requirements due to non-transparent ownership structures of banks. Credit risk is a concern given the rapid credit growth and concentrated loan exposures, particularly to related parties. Increased competition is putting pressure on interest margins while increased cost and recent decline in trading income further erode banks' profitability.

The deposit insurance system (DIS) has been introduced in 2004–05. All deposits up to Rub100,000 in commercial bank included into DIS will be insured. The authorities have seen the DIS not only as a key element in leveling the playing field, but also as a vehicle to effectively re-license the banking sector and weed out weak banks. About 1,150 banks applied for authorization to join the deposit insurance scheme. By the end of 2005, 930 banks were included into the system.

Banks dominate Russian debt market. They account for about 70 percent of the domestic government bond market, 50–60 percent of the sub-sovereign debt and more than 40 percent of the corporate bond market. Banks play an active role as underwriters of regional and corporate debt.

Capital Markets and Non-Bank Financial Institutions

Russian capital markets and institutional investors have undergone remarkable development and growth since end 2000. On the supply side, the equity market capitalization grew rapidly not only as a result of price appreciation of outstanding securities, but also as a result of additional securities admitted for trading on local exchanges, as well as IPOs and SPOs primarily on international markets. Equity market capitalization expanded from its 1.2 trillion rubles (or 17 percent of GDP) 2000 basis to about 6.9 trillion rubles (or 41 percent of GDP) by end 2004. In 2005, new companies admitted for trading as a result of energy sector reforms along with the surge in price of blue chips (primarily Gazprom) led to unprecedented growth, raising market capitalization to an estimated 70 percent of GDP. A number of Russian companies went through IPO in 2004–05, raising US$0.3 billion in 2004 and US$0.2 billion in 2005. The number and size of Russian public offerings on international markets (primarily on London) was substantially higher (US$0.3 for IPOs and US$1.9 billion for SPOs in 2004 and US$4 billion though IPOs in 2005) The IPO on international markets are expanding beyond the more traditional large extractive industry and energy sector corporate issuers to include smaller retail, pharmaceutical and internet/media companies.

The domestic corporate bond market has also undergone substantial development both in size and quality expanding from mere Rub38.9 billion by end 2000 (0.5 percent of GDP) to Rub16.7 billion (2.2 percent of GDP) by end 2005. Corporate bonds are becoming an important source of financing for mid and large corporate issuers in various industries. Just in 2005, over Rub270 billion (US$9.7 billion) were raised by Russian companies through corporate bonds. The duration of the corporate bonds placed increased from less than one year in 2000 to about four years in 2005.

Corporate debt began to compete with bank loan financing. Individual banks are small relative to large Russian industrial enterprises, while the industrial enterprises are in turn very large relative to corporate structures elsewhere. Banks are individually not able to supply adequate debt financing for the large companies and loan syndication is rare. Russian companies also have a considerable capacity to borrow since they have a relatively low leverage.

The domestic government bond market has experienced major restructuring in 2003–05, with partial substitution of the external debt with domestic debt and streamlining of Government bond series into fewer, larger issues). The sub-sovereign bond market has grown vigorously since its re-emergence in 2001 and has now become the largest sub-sovereign bond market among emerging economies with Rub161 billion (equivalent to US$5.6 billion) bonds outstanding by end 2005.

On the demand side, institutional investors grew as well. Since 2000, the Net Asset Value (NAV) of local Unit Investment Funds (PIFs) and Joint-Stock Investment Funds (AIFs) combined increased Rub8.8 billion by end 2000 to Rub235.8 billion by end 2005. The pension reserves of the Non-state Pension Funds (NSPF) grew from Rub15.6 billion by end 2000 to over Rub200 billion by end 2005. Since the introduction of the multi-pillar pension system in 2002, the funded part of the Second Pillar grew to Rub239.9 billion, although only Rub5.9 billion were transferred to the private sector asset management companies and the non-state pension funds by end 2005.

The role of domestic institutional investors is growing both on equity and bond market. The investor base on the equity market includes a large share of global investment funds with longer-term investment strategies.

Table 3: Capital Market (Supply side) (billions of rubles)

	2000	2001	2002	2003	2004	2005
Government Bonds Outstanding, Nominal	230.1	160.1	217.0	314.6	557.6	721.6
as % of GDP	3.2	1.8	2.0	2.4	3.3	3.3
Subnational Bonds Outstanding, Nominal	11.24	23.51	34.92	83.18	128.25	161.07
as % of GDP	0.2	0.3	0.3	0.6	0.8	0.7
Equity Market Capitalization	1115.0	2499.0	3650.0	5807.0	6867.0	15212.5
as % of GDP	15.3	27.9	33.7	43.8	40.4	70.2
Corporate Bonds Outstanding, Nominal	38.9	67.2	108.9	159.8	267.6	481.3
as % of GDP	0.5	0.8	1.0	1.2	1.6	2.2
Derivatives, Open Contracts	0.0	0.5	1.2	2.2	7.9	
as % of GDP	0.0	0.0	0.0	0.0	0.0	

Source: WB calculations (CBR for government bonds, Cbonds for subnational and corporate bonds, EMDB for equity, FSFM for Derivatives).

Despite the above developments, some important market weaknesses and impediments remain. On the supply side, the equity market remains concentrated among few issuers in terms of capitalization, free-float and turnover. The high transaction cost and risk of domestic trading, along with continuing perceptions of poor protection of investors' rights, have been driving secondary trading abroad (primarily to the London market). Derivatives' trading is limited due to the absence of the solid legal base and no legal protection of derivatives transactions. On the demand side, the role of domestic institutional investors (investment funds, pension funds, and insurance companies) remains marginal in compare with other domestic and foreign investors. The settlement and clearing infrastructure remains fragmented and full DVP clearing with guaranteed execution of trading is not available on domestic exchange platforms.

Table 4: Capital Market (Demand side) (billions of rubles)

	2000	2001	2002	2003	2004	2005
Banking sector assets	2362.5	3159.7	4145.3	5600.7	7136.9	9750.3
as % of GDP	32.3	35.3	38.3	42.3	42.0	45.0
Securities held by banks	473.2	562	779.9	1002.2	1086.9	1539.4
as % of GDP	6.5	6.3	7.2	7.6	6.4	7.1
Investment funds	8.8	11.5	14.6	80.6	113.3	235.8
as % of GDP	0.1	0.1	0.1	0.6	0.7	1.1
Pension reserves (NSPF)	15.6	33.6	51.4	91.7	169.8	198.9
as % of GDP	0.2	0.4	0.5	0.7	1.0	0.9
Pillar 2 Pension (Funded portion)			33.7	81.5	158.9	239.9
as % of GDP			0.3	0.6	0.9	1.1
Pillar 2 Funds managed by SPF and VEB			33.7	81.5	155.7	234
as % of GDP			0.3	0.6	0.9	1.1
Pillar 2 Funds managed by NSPF						2.1
as % of GDP						0.0
Pillar 2 Funds managed by asset management companies					3.2	3.8
as % of GDP					0.0	0.0
Gross Premiums, Insurance companies	170.1	291.2	329.9	446.8	470.5	
as % of GDP	2.3	3.3	3.0	3.4	2.8	

Legal and Regulatory Framework for Securities Markets

Recent Evolution

The foundation for the current legal system for the securities market began to form in mid 90s, starting with the establishment of the Federal Commission for Securities Market (FCSM) and the adoption of the Civil Code (Part I) in late 1994, followed by the establishment of the norms for joint stock companies and securities markets in the Joint Stock Companies Law (JSC Law) enacted in 1995 and the Securities Market Law (SML) enacted in 1996. In 1998, the law regulating the issuance of government and sub-sovereign securities, as well as the law regulating activities of the non-state pension funds was enacted. Following the crisis of 1998, the government developed the Law on Protection of Investors' Rights that was enacted in spring of 1999. In the late 2001, the Investment Funds law regulating activities of investment funds was adopted. The development and adoptions of the new Budget Code in 2002 enforced strict prudential control over finance of Russian regions, which helped to reduce credit risk of the sub-sovereign bonds in the re-emerged after the crisis sub-sovereign bond market.

It must be noted that in the 90s the securities market were developing ahead of the legislation. As a result, many laws enacted in mid- and late 1990s mostly aimed to fill in the existing gaps, rather than focusing on the establishment of the comprehensive legal system. Many laws were first adopted with major inconsistencies, contradictions, and gaps, which had to be addressed through a number of amendments in the course of 2001–04. For instance, the Securities Market Law has been amended and expended five times since the enactment of the law in 1996, with the last amendments enacted in July 2005. Some area of securities market activities are still not covered by Federal laws or Presidential Decrees and are governed by specific instructions or letters issued by related ministries.

By mid-2005, the following core legal documents have been enacted by the Government of Russia (GOR):

Federal Codes

- The Civil Code of Russian Federation (Part 1) of November 1994 (last amended in July 2005)
- The Civil Code of Russian Federation (Part 2) of January 1996 (last amended in July 2005)
- The Budget Code of Russian Federation, 145-FZ of July 1998 (last amended in May 2005)
- The Tax Code of Russian Federation (Part 1) of July 1998 (last amended in July 2005)
- The Tax Code of Russian Federation (Part 2) of August 2000 (last amended in July 2005)
- The Civil Procedural Code of Russian Federation of November 2002 (last amended in July 2005)
- Criminal Code of May 1996 (last amended in July 2005)
- Administrative Code of December 2001 (last amended in August 2005)

Federal Laws

- Federal Law # 208-FZ "On Joint Stock Companies" of December 1995 (last amended in December 2004)
- Federal Law # 39-FZ "On Securities Market" of April 1996 (last amended in June 2005)
- Federal Law # 48-FZ "On Bills and Promissory Notes of March 1997
- Federal Law # 136-FZ "On Specifics of Issue and Distribution of Government and Municipal Securities" of July 1998 (last amended in July 2005)
- Federal Law #75-FZ "On Non State Pension Funds" of May 1998 (last amended in May 2005)
- Federal Law # 46-FZ "On Protection of Rights and Legitimate Interests of Investors in Securities Market" of March 1999 (last amended in June 2005)
- Federal Law # 102-FZ "On Mortgage (collateral)" of July 1998 (last amended in December 2004)
- Federal Law # 127-FZ on Bankruptcy of October 2002 (last amended in December 2004)
- Federal Law # 156-FZ "On Investment Funds" of November 2001 (last amended in June 2004)
- Federal Law # 111-FZ "On Investment of the Accumulative Portion of the Labor (mandatory) Pension in Russian Federation" of July 2002 (last amended in May 2005)
- Federal Law #173-FZ "On Currency Regulation and Control" of December 2003 (last amended in July 2005)
- Federal Law # 152-FZ "On Mortgage Securities" of November 2003 (last amended in December 2004)

■ Federal Law # 117-FZ "On Accumulative Mortgage System for Supply of Housing for Military Personnel" of August 2004

■ Federal Law #3119 "On Commodity Exchanges" (Last amended in June 2004)

Other Regulations

■ Federal Decree # 6251 "On Activities of Trade Organizers in Securities Market" of December 2004

■ Federal Decree #05-5/pz-n "On the Establishment of Norms for Information Disclosure by Issuers of Marketable Securities" of March 2005

■ FSFM Order #05-5/pz-n "On Rules for Information Disclosure by Issuers of Publicly Traded Securities" of March 2005

■ FSFM Order #06-5/pz-n "On Standards of Security Issuance and Prospectus Registration" of March 2005

Significant Progress Had been Made by in Recent Years in Filling the Gaps in the Securities Market Legal Framework. Particularly Noteworthy are the Adoption of

■ Development of the FFMS Financial Market Development Strategy (expected to be adopted by GOR in February 2006);

■ Introduction of stricter listing and trade reporting requirements for Exchanges and market participants in closer line with international standards;

■ Development and adoption of secondary legislation to complete the legal base for mortgage-backed securities;

■ Introduction of legal provisions to improve regulation of the pension funds industry in relation to investment of second pillar mandatory pension funds;

■ Development of legal provisions to the Securities Market Law and the Joint-Stock Company Law to improve the legal framework for domestic IPOs (expected to be adopted in early 2006);

■ Amendments to the Securities Market Law to establish a legal base for short-term corporate bonds equivalent to commercial papers (expected to be adopted in 2006);

■ Amendments to the Securities Market Law to enable issuance and trading of Russian Depositary Receipts on foreign stocks on domestic exchanges (expected to be adopted in 2006).

At the same time, the legal and regulatory framework is far from completion and requires substantial improvements, in particular, in the areas of shareholder's rights protection, security issuance and trading, clearing and settlement, prevention of inside trading, legal foundations for derivatives and asset-backed securities.

Five self-regulatory organizations (SROs) have been created in Russian financial market: The National Association of Stock and Bond Market Participants (NAUFOR), the National Securities Market Association (NFA), the Professional Association of Registrars, Transfer Agents and Depositaries (PARTAD), the National League of Asset Management Companies (NLU), and the Professional Institute for Stock Placement and Circulation (PROFI). Although self-regulatory organizations play a role in legislation drafting and delivering opinions of market participants to authorities, their regulatory and supervisory role is limited. In addition, the division of SROs by sectors dilutes their effectiveness. Moreover, NAUFOR, NFA, and PROFI practically enroll members from the same industry and effectively dilute the effectiveness of each SRO. The stock exchanges in Russia do not have self-regulatory organization status, although they have membership requirements and follow the activities of their members in the market in coordination with the regulator to ensure market integrity and efficiency.

Key Impediments and Priorities Going Forward

Overall, the current securities market legislation has one fundamental problem. Russia has a continental law system and most of the financial market legislation is based on the Civil Code. However, the Securities Market Law was first drafted based on the example of US-type securities market legislation, which is precedent-based. This created a misalignment of the Securities Market Law with the rest of Russian legislation (including banking legislation). The current legal framework for securities markets consists of many individual and sometimes inconsistent legislative acts. It would be advisable to restructure this framework into fewer but mutually consistent legislative acts, focusing laws on general regulatory principles and leaving detailed regulations for specific regulatory acts that can be amended more easily.

Going forward, FSFM proposes to address key legal and regulatory impediments to market development by focusing on the following reform priorities:

■ *Development of the legal base for derivatives.* The Russian derivatives market is extremely limited due to the absence of a sound legal base for market functioning. Under current legislation, the parties' rights and obligations in transaction with derivatives, as well as accounting and taxation of derivative transactions are not clearly defined. The Civil Code currently treats transactions with derivatives as "gambling transactions" (wagers), which are not subject to legal protection under the Code. In order to develop the derivatives market, the Government has to adopt necessary amendments to the Civil Code, and adopt the draft Law on Derivatives.

■ *Development of exchange trade regulation.* At present, exchange trading in Russia is fragmented and poorly capitalized. Russian trading floors lag behind major international trading floors in terms of turnover, liquidity, and pricing efficiency. Russian exchanges still operate on expensive terms of pre-depositing and pre-funding, while delivery vs. payment (DVP) method is used on all major international exchanges. Due to the above inefficiency of the domestic infrastructure, a considerable part of Russian equities is traded abroad, particularly in London, in form of depositary receipts. In the absence of the legal base and limited infrastructure, Russian investors hedge most of the Russian securities risk through derivatives traded on international markets. To address these problems, FSFM intends to develop a special Law "On Exchanges and Exchange Activities" which would streamline and improve organization of trading for stocks, bonds, currencies and commodities on futures. The law would clarify the legal status of exchanges, set clear shareholder structure requirements and corporate governance system to make domestic exchanges more transparent and attractive for investors. The regulator also plans to pass certain regulatory powers to exchanges in relation to traders and issuers.

■ *Adoption of Law "On Inside Information and Market Manipulation."* Currently, there are no effective penalties for inside trading and price manipulation. The existing legislation does not define "insider" and "inside information". The Law "On Securities Markets" contains a definition of "office information" and prohibits trading on it. However, the existing definition of inside information is inadequate and the existing penalty for inside trading is limited only to small fine insufficient to stop inside trading practices. "Price Manipulation" that usually goes along with inside trading is also poorly regulated. The Law "On Securities Markets" does contain a definition of "price manipulation" and related penalties. However, the existing definition makes it difficult to prove market participant guilty of such violation. No fines are provisioned for price manipulation. The possible penalty is limited only to suspension or canceling of professional licenses of market participant, which is not always adequate. Neither inside trading nor price manipulation provision criminal liability. As a result, inside trading and price manipulation activities are very common in Russia. To ban these common practices of violations, FSFM proposes to adopt a special law "On Inside Information and Market Manipulation" with related amendments in the law "On Securities Market" and the RF Code on Administrative Violations and the RF Criminal Code. The already drafted law provision administrative and criminal liability for the certain types of inside trading and price manipulation violations.

■ *Clear regulation of corporate mergers.* Current gaps in the corporate and securities market legislation are used by imprudent investors for gaining control over a target company at an unreasonably low price through various abuses of the law. Unfriendly and unfair corporate takeovers are becoming a common practice. These abuses undermine regular investors' trust in Russian stock market investments. At the moment, Article 80 of the Securities Market Law does set specific responsibilities for entities that intend to purchase 30 percent or more of voting shares in the joint-stock company. However, the existing regulations are not sufficient. The FSFM intend to introduce additional amendments to the Securities Market Law and the Law on Joint-Stock Companies in order to introduce more effective regulation for corporate takeovers and the enforcement for related regulations. More clear and fair rules for corporate takeovers would raise investors' confidence in the stock market investment and would improve overall investment climate in Russia.

■ *Adoption of legislation on securitization.* Asset-backed securities that are actively issued and traded on developed markets do not exist in Russia due to the lack of the relevant securitization legislation. Under current Securities Market Law, financial asset is recognized as a security only if there is a direct indication of this security in the law. At the moment, most Securitization structures are not possible in Russia due to the absence of Securitization Law and limitations of the existing laws. The adoption of the Loan Mortgage Securities in 2004 is the first step accomplished by regulator and the government toward the development of asset-backed securities sector. The next step would be the adoption of the Securitization Law and amendments to the existing legislation to allow securitization structures in Russia. At the moment, FSFM is drafting the Law on Securitization. Apart from the Securitization law, it would be necessary to amend the Civil Code, Tax Code, the Law on Joint Stock Companies, The Law On Securities Markets, The Law on Insolvency (Bankruptcy), the Law on Foreign Currency Regulation, and the Law on Banks and Banking Activity. To adopt the complete legal base for securitization, FSFM would seek support and approval from CBR (banking regulator) since CBR would have to introduce the necessary amendments to the Law on Foreign Currency Regulation and the Law on Banks and Banking Activity.

Market Infrastructure

Recent Evolution

The Russian securities market's trading, settlement and clearing infrastructure was first built in mid 90s during the GKO and post-privatization stock market euphoria. The system was targeted primarily for non-resident investors, who were investing in Russia through offshore companies without actually brining funds into Russia to minimize Russian jurisdiction, operational, and custodian risks. In this system broker rather than investor carried those risks. Thus, each Russian exchange and its brokers began to build its own settlement and clearing system. Since brokers carried most risks, capitalization of major brokers increased, while the capitalization of the system remained low.

The Russian securities market's trading, settlement and clearing infrastructure has consolidated in the last few years, but, overall, still remains fragmented and undercapitalized. Trading in corporate securities is organized on several markets (MICEX, RTS, St. Petersburg Stock Exchange, St. Petersburg Currency Exchange), which compete with each other for attraction of investors and propose their own infrastructure elements (NDC, DCC, RDK, RDC).[1]

The Central Depositary (CD), Central Settlement System (CSS) and Central Clearing System (CCS) have not been established. The state unitary enterprise "The Central Fund for Storage and Processing of the Capital Market Information—the Central Depositary" established in 1997 does not play the role of the Central Depositary for securities market.

---

1. National Depository Center (NDC)—Moscow Interbank Currency Exchange (MICEX)
   Depositary Clearing Center (DCC)—RTS Stock Exchange (RTS)
   Settlement Depositary Company (RDK)—St. Petersburg Stock Exchange (SPSE)
   Settlement Depositary Center (RDC)—St. Petersburg Currency Exchange (SPCEX).

Table 5: Markets for Russian Securities

Type of Securities	Instrument	Market
Government Securities	**Denominated in RUB**	
	RF MOF Zero-Coupon bills (GKO)	MICEX GSM Section (non in circulation since end 2004)
	RF MOF Bonds with floating or fixed coupons (OFZ)	MICEX GSM Section and since mid 2005-OTC
	Central Bank of Russia bonds (OBR)	MICEX GSM Section
	Denominated in foreign currency RF MOF domestic foreign currency bonds (OVVZ)	International OTC
	RF Eurobonds	International OTC/MICEX
Sub-sovereign Securities	**Denominated in RUB**	
	Bonds issued by RF Subjects and municipalities (with the exception of St. Petersburg bonds)	MICEX SE
	St. Petersburg regional bonds	St. Petersburg Currency Exchange (SPCEX)
	Denominated in foreign currency Eurobonds issued by RF Subjects	International OTC
Corporate Securities	**Denominated in RUB**	
	Stocks	MICEX/RTS/OTC
	Corporate Bonds	MICEX/OTC
	Denominated in foreign currency Depositary receipts on Russian stocks	LSE/NYSE/Deutsche Bourse/NASDAQ
	Stocks of foreign SPV representing Russian companies	LSE
	Corporate Eurobonds	International OTC
Derivatives	**Denominated in RUB**	
	Futures and Options on blue chip stocks and stock indices	FORTS (Futures and Options on RTS),
	Denominated in foreign currency Foreign derivatives on Russian depositary receipts	CBOE, CBOT

The Russian securities market operates mostly as a "dematerialized" system, with the only exception of the domestic foreign currency bonds issued by MOF. Russian equities and bonds are not represented by paper certificates, but are recorded in a book-entry system. Table 5 shows the main market places for Russian securities.

Exchange Trading

Organized securities trading in Russia has consolidated in the last few years primarily into two major markets: the Moscow Interbank Currency Exchange Group (MICEX Group) which accounts for the largest share of the domestic organized securities trading, and the

Russian Trading System Group (RTS Group), which accounts for the rest of the onshore organized trading. MICEX Group consists of the Moscow Interbank Currency Exchange (MICEX), MICEX Stock Exchange, and some regional exchanges. RTS Group consists of the RTS Classic Market, RTS Stock Exchange, St. Petersburg Stock Exchange, Futures and Options on RTS (FORTS) system for derivatives. Government bonds are traded exclusively on the government bonds section on MICEX. Sub-sovereign bonds are traded primarily on MICEX Stock Exchange (over 90 percent of turnover), with the exception of St. Petersburg bonds, which are traded only on St. Petersburg Currency Exchange (SPCEX). Corporate bonds are traded primarily on MICEX (nearly 100 percent of organized trading). Most stocks are traded on MICEX (over two thirds of organized trading in 2005) and RTS (the rest of turnover). Prior to 2006, the shares of Gazprom gas monopoly were traded mostly on St. Petersburg Stock exchange (part of RTS Group) and settled through RTS infrastructure. Starting from 2006, Gazprom shares are listed and traded both on MICEX and RTS. Stock Options and Futures are traded primarily on Futures and Options trading platform on RTS (FORTS) (nearly 100 percent of organized trading in the equity derivatives).

Most regional exchanges have a remote access to electronic trading system of MICEX and are part of MICEX Group. The Moscow Stock Exchange (MSE) that used to be the main trading platform for Gazprom shares prior to 2002 has become inactive while most Gazprom trading shifted to Stock Exchange St. Petersburg (part of RTS Group).

MICEX Group. MICEX was established in January of 1992 as currency exchange in the form of close joint-stock company by Central Bank of Russia, Association of Russian Banks, Government of Moscow, Sberbank and the leading commercial banks of Russia. Starting from July of the same year, CBR began to establish official ruble exchange rate based on the results of MICEX trading. Starting from 1993, CBR began to trade government securities market organizing auctions and secondary trading in government short term discount bonds (GKO) on MICEX. Starting from 1996, derivatives began to trade on MICEX. Starting from 1997, MICEX began to trade stock of the most liquid blue-chip companies, such as Mosenergo, Rostelecom, Nornikel, and RAO UES. During the GKO boom of 1996–98, MICEX developed a well functioning trading infrastructure for government securities trading, with major commercial banks participating in the trading. After the GKO market collapse in 1998, government bonds market become inactive. At the same time, when corporate bond market began to emerge in Russia in 1999, MICEX naturally become the market place for corporate bonds, since all related trading infrastructure was already in place. By 2003, most corporate and sub-sovereign bonds were placed and traded on MICEX. With the decline in the volume of foreign investors trading on RTS and increased activity of the domestic investors, MICEX evolve into the leading trading platform for stocks.

Currently, MICEX Group is the largest securities trading, clearing and settlement infrastructure complex in Russia. As of the end of 2004, MICEX accounted for 90 percent of organized securities trading in Russia, nearly 100 percent trading in ruble corporate bonds and about 80 percent of the domestic trading in stocks.

MICEX Group organizes trading in the following segments of the financial market:

- *Currencies Market.* Foreign exchange trading accounts for the largest portion of MICEX trade volume, primarily U.S. dollar trading. Since 1992, CBR establishes the official US$/Rub exchange rate based U.S. dollar trading results on MICEX. In 2004, currencies annual turnover reached Rub10.05 trillion (US$350 billion), growing more than twofold since 2003. This was a result of the merger of the Unified trading System (UTS) and the System of Electronic Lot Trades in currency (SELT), which completed the unification of the national currency market in Russia. The monthly turnover in currencies increased to US$58.2 billion in December and exchange trading of currencies increased to 83 percent from 79 percent in 2003. U.S. dollar trading accounts for 69 percent of the total currency trade volume. U.S. dollar swaps account for 30 percent, with only about 1 percent of trade volume accounting for other currencies trading.

■ *Government Securities Market.* Since 1993, MICEX was the only exchange authorized to organize trading in ruble denominated government securities (GKOs/OFZs). In 1996–1998, GKO turnover to bonds outstanding grew to 200-400 percent. After the collapse of the GKO market, the government bonds trading dropped sharply and stayed below 20 percent in 1999–2002. Only starting from 2003, government bonds trading picked up. Starting from 2004, MICEX created an official Government Securities Section (GSM) for government securities placement auctions, secondary trading, and REPO transactions. Members of the GSM are dealers of the GKO/OFZ market. The list of securities admitted for trading on the Government Securities Section includes RF Ministry of Finance ruble bonds (GKO-OFZs), Central Bank of Russia ruble bonds (OBRs), RF Eurobonds, and the City of Moscow ruble bonds. In addition MICEX provides access for credit institutions to Central Bank deposits. In 2004, the total annual turnover of government securities reached Rub1,352 trillion (US$46.8 billion), including Rub620.4 billion (US$21.4 billion) in REPO and reverse REPO transactions. The most active segments of the government securities market are OFZs secondary trading and Central Bank REPO. Inter-dealer REPO became possible since late 2003.

■ *The Non-Government Securities Market (NGSM).* The stock market component of MICEX organizes trading in stocks (since 1997), corporate and sub-sovereign bonds (since 1999), and investment fund shares (since 2003). In 2004, MICEX succeeded in restructuring the stock market component of its business in compliance with the law. The MICEX Group transferred listing and trading of all corporate and sub-sovereign securities from the Stock Market Section of MICEX to the newly founded MICEX Stock Exchange (MICEX SE), which obtained appropriate stock exchange license from the FSFM. Currently the organization of trading in the non-government securities is distributed between the MICEX and MICEX SE in the following way:

● MICEX SE organizes listing and trading (since January 11, 2005).
● MICEX provides clearing, settlement and depositary functions for securities trading on MICEX SE. In 2004 the total trading volume of the non-government securities market on MICEX grew by 44 percent in 2004 to Rub4351.18 billion (equivalent of US$151.2 billion). The secondary trading in stocks accounted for Rub2778.85 billion (US$96.6 billion) or 64 percent of the total turnover and the secondary trading in corporate and sub-sovereign bonds—for Rub761.21 billion (US$26.5 billion) or 17 percent of the total turnover.

■ *Derivatives Market.* MICEX main derivatives product is FX futures, which are traded in the MICEX Derivatives (Standard Contract) Market Section. Due to the absence of the solid legal foundations for derivatives, the derivatives turnover is low and accounted only to Rub13 billion (US$0.46 billion) in 2004. In 2002–03, MICEX has also organized trading in stock futures, but the enactment of the RF Federal Securities Commission's Decree #03-54/ps of 26.12.03 negatively impacted that market. According to this decree, as of January 1, 2005, trading in derivatives on stocks, bonds and related indexed is only allowed on stock exchanges. MICEX is planning to develop this market once the relevant infrastructure will be created as part of the MICEX SE.

■ *Commodity Market.* The MICEX is currently trying to develop commodities market jointly with the National Mercantile Exchange (NAMEX). In 2004, NAMEX performed functions of the administrator of the trading system during government intervention in the grain market in 2004, using the technological services of the MICEX. MICEX plans to continue cooperation with the NAMEX in further development of the commodities market.

MICEX Group is a closed joint-stock company incorporated in Russia. Based on the Consolidated Financial Statement of MICEX for 2004 under IFRS, the largest shareholders of the MICEX Group are CBR (29 percent), International Moscow Bank (12 percent), and Vnesheconombank (11 percent). Other shares are owned by the 13 Russian banks (incl. Sberabank RF, Vneshtorgbank, Rosbank, Bank of Moscow) each holding less than 10 percent of shares. MICEX has three principle subsidiaries: (1) Closed Joint Stock Company "Stock Exchange MICEX", (2) Non-commercial organization—Closed Joint-Stock Company "Settlement House of MICEX," and (3) Non-commercial partnership "National Depository Center."

Stock Exchange MICEX lists and organizes trading in stocks, corporate and subsovereign bonds, and investment funds shares, while MICEX Group organizes clearing and trading support of transaction on Stock Exchange MICEX. Settlement House of MICEX is used for cash settlement of MICEX trades. National Depository Center offers securities settlement and depository services to MICEX clients. In addition to the principle subsidiaries, MICEX Groups includes several regional exchanges connected into MICEX trading system, the National Commodities Exchange (NAMEX) that trade commodities with technical support of MICEX, and IT Company "E-stock" for support of the MICEX system hardware and software. All MICEX trades are settled in ruble only with pre deposit fund and securities settlement system.

CJSC MICEX holds CBR licenses for foreign currency trading, FCSM licenses for securities trading and clearing activities, and the Commodity Exchange Commission licenses for the organization of trades on the derivatives' market. Stock Exchange MICEX hold stock exchange license issued by FSFM in 2004. Settlement House of MICEX has license for banking operations issued by Bank of Russia in 1996 and a license for depository activity issued by FSFM in 2004. National Depository Center holds a license for depository and clearing activities issued by the Federal Commission on Securities Market in 2000.

The RTS Group. Russian Trading System Group is the second largest securities exchange in Russia. It accounts for about 20 percent of domestic turnover in Russian stocks, and 100 percent turnover in futures and options on stocks.

RTS was set up in 1995 as a screen based PORTAL trading system, the same as used by US NASDAQ. In 1998, RTS developed and adopted more advance trading hardware and software developed in-house. Originally, RTS specialized on stocks trading with settlement in US$. Within the years, RTS has diversified its range of trading services into derivatives and fixed income product and introduced ruble settlement. In cooperation with St. Petersburg Stock Exchange, RTS organized trading; clearing and settlement for GAZPROM shares and by 2004 become the main trading platform for the shares of the gas monopoly.

As of 2004, RTS Group is organized in the form of the Non-Profit Partnership "RTS Stock Exchange" (NP RTS SE) which consist of Open Joint Stock Company "RTS Stock Exchange" (OJSC RTS SE), the non-profit partnership "St. Petersburg Stock Exchange" (NP STSE), Closed Joint Stock Company "Clearing Center RTS" (CJSC RTS Clearing Center), Limited Partnership—Non-commercial Organization "RTS Settlement House," the Non-Profit Partnership "Depository Clearing Center"(DKK), Closed Joint Stock Company "Depository Clearing Center" (DKK) and the Closed Joint Stock IT Company "Skrin" (SKRIN).

The RTS Group organizes trading in equities, bonds, investment fund shares, futures and options on shares. Securities trading on RTS Group is broken down into the following markets:

- *RTS Classic Market:* A quote-driven non-anonymous market for equities, corporate and sub-sovereign bonds, and investment funds shares with U.S. dollar or ruble settlement on the DVP T+ 4 or Free Delivery from T+ 0 to T+ 30 terms. The NP RTS SE organizes trading, while clearing is organized by the NP RTS SE for ruble DVP settlement and by the DCC for U.S. dollar DVP settlement. Cash settlement is done by any bank with JP Morgan Chase bank accounting for about 30 percent of settlement. Any depositary or registrar conducts securities re-registration with the DCC accounting for 90 percent.
- *RTS Stock Exchange:* An order driven double-auction anonymous market for stocks, bonds, and investment funds settled in rubles with full preliminary deposition of assets on T+0 terms. The OJSC RTS SE organizes trading, while the NP RTS SE conducts clearing. NKO RTS Settlement House is used for cash settlement. Securities re-registered at the DCC.
- *Gazprom Shares:* An order-driven anonymous auction for ordinary Gazprom shares settled in rubles with full preliminary deposition of assets on T+ 0 terms. Trading is organized on the NP "St. Petersburg Stock Exchange", while the NP RTS SE manages clearing. Cash settlement is managed by the NKO RTS Settlement House. Purchase securities are registered at the RDK (Settlement depositary for Gazprom).
- *RTS Board:* The system used for indicative quotation on the OTC market for equities and bonds.
- *Futures and Options on RTS (FORTS):* Futures and options on stock trading, anonymous auctions with ruble settlement, full preliminary deposition of margin. Trading is organized by the NP RTS SE, while clearing is managed by the RTS Clearing Center. Cash settlement is managed by the RTS Settlement House.

Purchase securities are registered at the DCC, with the exception of the Gazprom derivatives registered at the RDK.

■ *NQS Bills:* The system used for indicative quotation on the OTC market of veksel

Table 6: MICEX Turnover (billions of rubles)

GKO-OFZ	2000	2001	2002	2003	2004	2005
auctions (prim.)	15.3	45.36	79.26	112.18	134.64	182.317
secondary trades	184.92	155.42	147.95	269	338.98	496.76

OBR	2000	2001	2002	2003	2004	2005
auctions (prim.)	—	1.07	—	—	34.5	227.765
secondary trades	—	0.22	—	—	0	36.85

Eurobonds	2000	2001	2002	2003	2004	2005
secondary trades	—	—	0.36	1.1	5.97	0.62

Minfin bonds	2000	2001	2002	2003	2004	2005
secondary trades						0.02

REPO	2000	2001	2002	2003	2004	2005
GKO-OFZ*	—	—	28.38	732.75	756.63	1135.79
OBR*	—	—	—	—	81.72	661.84
Eurobonds	—	—	0	0	1.23	44.54

Regional Bonds	2000	2001	2002	2003	2004	2005
auctions (prim.)	—	3.1	11.6	41.91	53.06	51.97
secondary trades	—	6.6	24.18	118.12	326.22	559.52

Municipal Bonds	2000	2001	2002	2003	2004	2005
auctions (prim.)	—	—	0.49	1.56	1.97	24.32
secondary trades	—	—	0.45	2.37	11.79	1.65

Corporate Bonds	2000	2001	2002	2003	2004	2005
auctions (prim.)	29.55	24.7	47.64	78.41	141.12	259.45
secondary trades	5.57	33.4	72.34	251.69	422.44	901.52

Equities	2000	2001	2002	2003	2004	2005
auctions (prim.)	—	—	0.27	—	0.73	0.11
secondary trades	471.95	707.5	1144.26	2144.72	2778.85	3279.60

Investment Funds	2000	2001	2002	2003	2004	2005
secondary trades	—	—	—	0.1	0.14	1.54

REPO	2000	2001	2002	2003	2004	2005
Regional Bonds	—	—	0.69	23.82	114.7	267.43
Municipal Bonds	—	—	0.03	0.54	1.17	11.53
Corporate Bonds	—	—	3.13	50.76	151.89	390.75
Equities	—	—	72.33	310.15	345.56	745.33

Source: MICEX.

Settlement and Clearing

The settlement and clearing infrastructure remains fragmented and full DVP clearing with guaranteed execution of trading is not available on domestic exchange platforms. At present, Russian securities market infrastructure allows primarily two types of settlement: (1) pre-deposit funds and securities method and (2) "free delivery" or no depositing of funds and securities method. Pre-deposit funds and securities method makes local trading quite expensive, while free-delivery method having a high risk of non-payment of the buyer. RTGS is not implemented.

Due to the high transaction risks and high cost of the onshore trading liquidity in Russian securities, particularly equities, shifts abroad. In addition, substantial share of transactions between Russian market participants are settled abroad. Not only foreign investors, but also many Russian investors and intermediaries use foreign markets for indirect trading in Russian securities in the form of depositary receipts (ADR and GDR).

Depositories

It must be noted that according to Russian legislation the term "Depository" is broadly used to define various type of clearing and settlement institutions, which must be differentiated:

- *Settlement depository:* An organization alongside an exchange to facilitate settlement, temporary holding of stocks and registration (e.g. the National Depository Center and the Depository Clearing Company).
- *Custodian depository:* An organization used for the long-term safekeeping and administration of securities on behalf of clients (e.g. ROSBANK Depository—bank custodian).
- *Specialized depository:* Has characteristics of safekeeping and of supervision, more in the mode of trustee (for example, specialized depository for pension and investment funds).
- *Central depository:* A central reference database and guarantor of shareholder's rights. (Not established in Russia.)

Overall, the number of "Depositories" in Russia has expanded from 513 in 2000 to 737 in 2004, mainly due to the regional expansion of custodian services, which are now available practically everywhere throughout the territory of Russian Federation. Over the same time period, the settlement depositories experience major consolidation. Central Depository has not been established yet.

Settlement Depository (SD). The SD industry has consolidated in the last few years. Currently, Russian securities market has three major settlement depositories for most traded securities:

— *The National Depository Center (NDC)* serving MICEX trading floor and regional exchanges linked to MICEX.
— *The Depository and Clearing Company (Russian abbreviation: DKK)* serving RTS Classic Market and RTS Stock Exchange.

— *The Settlement Depository Company (Russian abbreviation: RDK)*, serving St. Petersburg Stock Exchange, specializing on Gazprom shares which are settled primarily through RDK.

All three settlement depositories are functioning well, but use different IT systems, not exactly compatible with each other. In recent years, the NDC and DCC were linked through "the bridge," inspired by the Euroclear-Cedel bridge, which enables brokers/dealers to transfer their securities holdings from their accounts with NDC to their accounts with DCC and vise versa.

The first step towards merger of the two major settlement depositories has been made— in 2004, when the NDC purchased 36.96 percent of shares of the DCC, with only 56.52 percent of the DCC shares remaining in the ownership of the RTS Group. Now NDC has 4 seats on the Board of Directors of the DCC. Currently, the NDC and the DCC are discussing the possibility of friendly merger in expectation of the establishment of the Central Depository on the basis of the merged NDC/DCC platform. The NDC has also purchased nearly 30 percent of shares in RDK, which gave it 2 seats on the Board of Directors of the RDK.

In addition to three major settlement depositories, there are two settlement depositories associated with the Moscow Stock Exchange (MSE) and St. Petersburg Currency Exchange (SPCEX):

— Settlement Depository Center (Russian abbreviation: RDC) specializing on the settlement of SPCEX trades, primarily St. Petersburg bonds.
— Depository Settlement Union (Russian abbreviation: DRS) specializing on the settlement of MSE trades.

Custodian Depositories. The number of custodian depositories increased from 500 levels in 2000 to 700 level in 2004 due to regional expansion of custodian services.

Specialized Depositories. Specialized depositories in Russia are serving the needs of the Pension Fund of Russia, non-state pension funds (NSPFs) and investment funds. The custodian services for the pension and investment funds can be provided only by the specialized depositories (around 25–29 depositories as of mid 2005).

Professional Market Participants (Financial Intermediaries)

Financial intermediaries have improved both in size in quality in recent years, while the industry has consolidated as a whole. Since 2002, the number of professional market

Table 7: Registrars and Depositories 1996–2004									
Number of	1996	1997	1998	1999	2000	2001	2002	2003	2004
Registrars	163	148	132	118	110	103	87	76	79
Depositories	6	172	112	133	513	698	759	804	737

Source: FSFM.

Table 8: Professional Market Participants

Licenses	1997	1998	1999	2000	2001	2002	2003	2004
Broker	393	372	261	205	252	246	98	91
Dealer	61	80	67	55	73	114	167	148
Broker/Dealer	1102	1030	825	637	632	680	368	432
Asset Management	0	11	16	43	68	127	80	120
Broker/Asset Mgmt	0	8	8	12	18	22	14	28
Dealer/Asset Mgmt	0	1	1	3	6	10	11	7
Broker/Dealer/Asset Mgmt	5	183	221	388	648	712	992	838
Total	1561	1685	1399	1343	1697	1911	1730	1664

Source: FSFM.

participants has been declining, while the ratio of universal companies that combine broker, dealer, and asset management activities has expanded. The average capital of the firms has increased. Typically for securities markets, the industry is quite concentrated. Out of 400 active professional market participants, 10 largest investment companies account for 80 percent of MICEX and RTS turnover, in compare with 70 percent of NYSE, 41 percent of NASDAQ, 80 percent of France, or 82 percent for WSE. (BCS report 2004). Most top foreign investment houses established or re-established their presence in Russia, including the banks that left Russia after the 1998 crisis.

As of the beginning of 2005, Russian investment intermediaries managed more than Rub311 billion or 4.4 percent of banking sector assets. Most of the resources managed by investment intermediaries are those accumulated by mutual funds and non-state pension funds (NSPF).

Key Impediments to Development

The existing system of record keeping in rights to securities has been formed by the middle 90s and now shows numerous deficiencies, which hamper the further development of the Russian capital market. The main deficiencies of the existing system of record keeping on the rights to securities are the following:

— High risk related to record keeping of the holder of registered securities (registrar risk);
— High degree of fragmentation of the existing capital market infrastructure (existence of several organized markets competing with each other for the clients and proposing its own settlement and clearing procedures);
— Low adaptability of the Russian record keeping system on rights to securities to the foreign registration and settlement systems;
— Pre-deposit funds and securities method makes local trading quite expensive, while free-delivery method having a high risk of non-payment of the buyer; and
— RTGS is not implemented.

The deficiencies of the system results in poor protection of rights for securities, risk of non-execution or under-execution of securities transactions, and high costs of trading and impediments to fair pricing. The fragmentation of the system forces market participants to be involved in different system of record keeping hampers transfer of securities and cash from one system to another. The low adaptability of the record keeping system does not allow foreign investors invest in Russian securities using their record keeping systems (including central depositaries). This leads to high costs of foreign investments into Russian securities and make direct investing unattractive.

The establishment of Central Depositary (CD) and centralized clearing would allow Russian exchange to trade on the partial pre-depositing of funds and securities with guaranteed execution of trade terms on the basis of "Delivery vs. Payment" (DVP). This would bring the efficiency of the settlement procedures to the international level. Both CSDs could be merged and strengthened to meet the needs of a growing market. The merged CSD would handle all type of securities (equities, bonds, derivatives).

Over time, the registrar industry will need to be rationalized. In the short-term, rationalization should be encouraged through increasing the requirements for registrars that serve publicly traded companies. In addition, the CSD could establish a common IT system with strong interface to the CSD system in order to service the registrar industry. Over the longer term, the CSD would become the mandatory registrar for publicly traded companies.

The post-trade transparency of RTS and MICEX are of reasonable standard to meet the needs of the Russian market. By contrast, the transparency of OTC trading is extremely low and not in line with international standards. While it is technically possible to report OTC trades to RTS, reporting by traders is voluntary. OTC trades are required to be reported to the regulator, but this takes place as part of periodical financial reporting and only for administrative purposes. A substantial share of OTC trades is reported to the settlement depositaries, but these data are not readily available to the public.

Reporting of OTC trades should be mandatory. End-of-day reporting could be established for a start, and reporting rules would be subsequently tightened in line with international standards. In addition, the regulator would need to establish procedures to ensure that traders comply with the reporting rules.

Key Priorities Going Forward

Key policy reform priorities for strengthening market institutions and infrastructure are as follows:

(i) Establish Central Settlement Depository (CSD). Amend the Law on Clearing to introduce centralized settlement and clearing, then capitalize the system.
(ii) Ensure effective RTGS system in place at least on MICEX and RTS; Enable DVP settlement to replace pre deposit fund and securities system.
(iii) Improve Registrar System in particular pushing for more consolidation of the registrars, evaluate linkages between CSD and the registrars, and evaluate CSD as registrar for listed securities.
(iv) Adopt international standards of risk management (CPSS/IOSCO among others).
(v) Develop adequate oversight capacity to ensure that risk management standards are met.

Government Bond Market

Recent Evolution

Since the emergence of the domestic government bond market in 1993, three types of ruble bonds have been issued and traded on the local market: (1) short-term zero-coupon state bonds (Russian abbreviation: GKO); (2) mid- and long-term state bonds with floating and fixed coupons (Russian abbreviation: OFZ); (3) and short-term zero-coupon Central Bank bonds (Russian abbreviation: OBR). GKOs and OFZs are issued by the Ministry of Finance for the purpose of financing budget deficit and refinancing the existing government debt. GKOs and OFZs are traded publicly and can be purchased by bank and non-bank financial institutions as well as individuals. OBRs are issued by the Central Bank to manage ruble liquidity. OBRs are sold only to banks.

Due to increasing duration of the government bonds in the last few years and the low MOF interest in short-term issues, GKO market has faded out in 2003–04. As of the end of 2004, there no GKO issues in circulation with the last issue redeemed in mid August 2004. At the same time, starting from the fall of 2004, Central Bank began to actively issue OBRs, placing nominal amount of Rub34.5 billion in 2004 and nominal amount of Rub227.8 billion in 2005. Since OBR is essentially a money market instrument used by CBR for liquidity management, we do not cover it further in this report.

Domestic Government Bonds

The August 1998 crisis marked a watershed in the short history of federal government securities. Prior to it, federal domestic debt, primarily in the form of short-term zero-coupon state bonds (GKOs),[2] was growing rapidly, peaking in 1997 at just over 20 percent of GDP.

---

2. By mid-1990s over 90 percent of domestic debt was securitized.

After the August 1998 default, domestic debt had shrunk both in absolute terms and as a share of GDP, as the GKOs were exchanged at a deep discount for medium-term government securities (OFZs). In the first three post-crisis years, new issuance was below redemption volumes. On the supply side, significantly improved fiscal discipline and tax revenues substantially reduced the borrowing requirements of the Federal government. Federal debt issuance picked up only in 2001–2002, buoyed by abundant liquidity in the banking system. In 2003–2004 new domestic issuance grew even stronger, following the government decision to gradually substitute part of external federal debt for domestic debt in order to revive domestic bond market.

Overall, the nominal value of OFZs outstanding grew from Rub506.1 billion by end of 2000 to Rub851.1 billion by end of 2005. At the same time, only portion of the total OFZs outstanding have been in circulation. At the end of 2000, only Rub228 billion out of Rub506.1 billion were traded in the secondary market. The rest of OFZ were hold by CBR. In 2000–02 period, CBR has actively purchased the outstanding government bonds, reducing the nominal value of OFZs in circulation from 43 percent of the total by end 2000 to 28–30 percent of the total in 2001–2002. The nominal value of OFZ in circulation dropped to the lowest level of Rub140.6 billion by end 2001. Only in 2003–2005, when government adopted a mid-term strategy for the revival of the government bond market, major portion of CBR portfolio was restructured and sold on the secondary market, increasing the share of OFZ in circulation to 85 percent of the total by end 2005 (See Table 9). In the favorable market conditions and excess banking sector liquidity, CBR has been permitted twice to sell portion of its portfolio in the open market in 2003–05.

Government bonds (OFZs) are placed and traded only on Government Securities Market section on MICEX. Since 2001, MOF has used very conservative approach in the bond placement. During market turmoil, it has stopped issuing papers completely. But whenever demand for bonds increased, it offered additional tranches on the secondary market. In the early years after the crisis, considerable amounts of the unsold portion of new issues were sold through the secondary market but the strong demand after 2001 has permitted the authorities to shift towards greater use of the auction mechanism. There are

Table 9: Government Bonds Outstanding, Billions of Rubles

	2000	2001	2002	2003	2004	2005
Government securities outstanding, nominal	531.8	511.1	654.7	663.7	756.8	851.2
Short-term bills (GKO)	3.1	19.5	18.8	2.7	0.0	0.02
Government Bonds (OFZ)	*506.1*	*470.5*	*624.2*	*649.3*	*756.8*	*851.1*
Non-market debt	22.7	21.1	11.7	11.6	0.0	0.03
Government securities in circulation, nominal	230.1	160.1	217.0	314.6	557.6	721.6
Short-term bills (GKO) in circulation	2.1	19.5	18.8	2.7	0.0	0.0
Government Bonds (OFZ) in circulation	228.0	140.6	198.2	311.9	557.6	721.6

Source: CBR.

still large additional placements through the secondary market, but this represent effectively the re-opening or the "tap" sale of longer term instruments in more favorable market conditions. These placements take place over a period of several months to more than a year for some issues and appear to reflect the authorities' policy of limiting the number of issues and controlling yields. By concentrating volume in a relatively smaller number of issues, the tradable amounts for each issue are increased, which supposed to facilitate trading in the secondary market.

Demand for Government securities has continued to far outstrip the supply, although most of the demand was originate in the state related institutions, primarily Sberbank and, since the introduction of the multipillar pension system—State Pension Fund. Trading in the secondary market remains limited. Average daily trading volumes fell sharply in 1998 and continued to decline for almost four years thereafter. There has been a noticeable increase since mid-2002, but overall activity is still a fraction of its pre-1999 level. The average monthly turnover of government bonds in circulation was below 8 percent in 2002–2005. This could partially be explained by the fact that the demand for government bonds is highly concentrated, with Sberbank holding more than half of outstanding issues. All State owned/ controlled banks (including Sberbank) accounts for about two thirds of GKO-OFZ trading.

OFZ yields have declined dramatically since 1998. From levels of up to 1,000 percent prior to 1998 GKO default, they fell to around 100 percent in early 1999 and continued on a downward trajectory that has brought them down under 12 percent yields for one year in 2003, turning yields negative in real term. Since then, average weight yield declined further to around 6–7 percent annual yields. The yields in real terms stayed below inflation level since January 2003.

Thanks to high oil prices and good fiscal discipline, the Russian government has constantly run surplus budget revenues and has not had to look for sources for covering budget deficit. Since the beginning of 2004, surplus revenues from oil tax have been stored in the established Stabilization Fund that has went over Rub520 billion by end of 2004 and reached Rub1460 billion by end of 2005. In this conditions, borrowing on the market become more of an option for than a necessity for Russian authorities. These favorable market conditions gave MOF an opportunity to revive the government bond market. The government tried to gave a new breath to the market in three steps: (1) reduce domestic interest rates (2) increase in duration of government bonds (3) improve liquidity of the outstanding issues. The first two goals have been more or less achieved. The YTM for one year bonds declined by about 15 percent since 2001 to around 5 percent by the end of 2004. The interest turned negative in real terms since 2003. The average duration of OFZs has increased substantially from about 1 year in 2002 to over 5 years in 2005. The benchmark issues have been established. Another planned action to boost market liquidity is the re-establishment of the primary dealer's institution on the government bond market.

While the first two goals were accomplished by the MOF, the liquidity is still a problem, primarily due to the current structure of demand for government securities, which concentrates mostly in the state related institutions. The demand, especially for longer maturities originates mostly from Sberbank[3] and the Pension Fund of Russia (including its

3. The 15-year issues are bought almost entirely by Sberbank.

Figure 5. OFZ Yields Dynamics

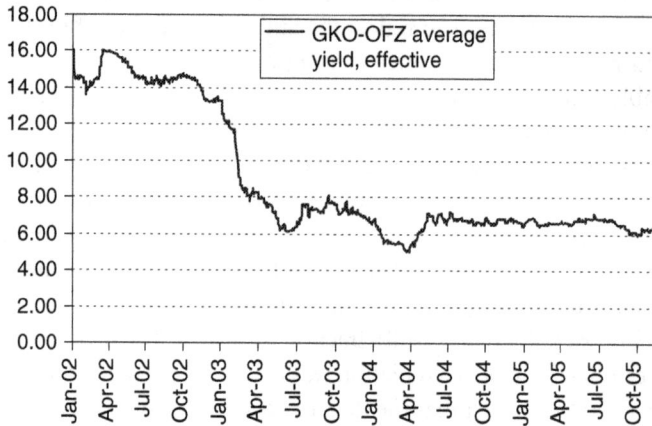

Source: CBR.

State Asset Management company managing PFR pensions—Russian abbreviation: GUK). For the purpose of investments into the state bonds, PFR and GUK can be considered as one institution since PFR manages state pensions accumulated within the current year and then transfer the funds to GUK that manages PFR portfolio accumulated from previous years (since 2002). Both Sberbank and PFR are very conservative buy and hold investors. According to Troika Dialog estimate, as of August 1, 2004, Sberbank accounted for about 61 percent of OFZ market, PFR (including state pension fund) for 13 percent of OFZs market, and only 26 percent of the market is hold by other investors. This, of course dramatically limits the liquidity of the OFZ market.

Sovereign Eurobonds

The sovereign Eurobond market has emerged in 1996 from the first US$1 billion issue and has grown rapidly to US$13.3 billion by end of July 1998. In the aftermath of the 1998 crisis, no new issues were placed until August 2000 when the largest issue Russia 30 and the third largest issue Russia 10 were placed as a result of the restructuring of the former Soviet Union debt, bring the Eurobond outstanding value to US$34.5 billion. At that time, outstanding Former Soviet Union debt amounting to US$22.2 billion in principal notes (PRINs), US$6.8 billion in interest arrears notes (IANs), and US$2.8 billion in past-due-interest (PDI) was swapped for US$18.3 billion in Russia 2030 Eurobonds and US$2.8 billion in Russia 2010 Eurobonds.[4] No new Eurobond issues have been placed since then. Most

---

4. In 2000, Russia signed an agreement with London Club members. Under the conditions of the agreement US$22.2 billion in Prins (bonds issued in exchange for old 1997 London Club principal), US$6.8 billion in Ians (bonds issued in exchange for interest arrears on 1997 London Club debt) was swapped for Russian Eurobonds maturing in 2030. Additionally, US$2.8 billion in past due interest (PDI) was converted to 9.5 percent cash payment and Russian Eurobonds Maturing in 2010.

Figure 6. JP Morgan EMBI+ Russia Spread, bp (2002–05)

Source: JP Morgan

outstanding Eurobonds were issued in U.S. dollars, with two 1997 bonds issued in DEM and one 1998 bond issued in ITL.

By the end 2004, sovereign Eurobonds market was comprised of six U.S. dollar-denominated bonds (US$32.9 billion in nominal value), and one euro-denominated (converted from DEM) bond (about US$0.8 billion in nominal value). The longest issue is Russia 2030. The largest and most actively traded issue is the benchmark Russia 2030 bond with outstanding amount of US$18.2 billion. Sovereign Eurobonds are the most liquid Russian securities that are traded by large foreign institutional investors and Russian banks on international OTC market.

Eurobonds Yields have declined sharply in the last three years. The EMBI+ Russia spread to U.S. dollar narrowed from 1137–1202 bps in December 2000 to 108–119 bps in December 2005.

Domestic Foreign Currency Bonds (Minfins)

Apart from regular government securities, the secondary market for Russian government bonds includes outstanding Government Domestic Foreign Currency Bonds (OVGVZ), or the so-called "Minfins." These are U.S. dollar denominated domestic bonds issued in the process of restructuring former USSR debt in early 1990s.

OVGVZ or "Minfins" are special type of bonds. "Minfins" are U.S. dollar-denominated domestic bonds issued in the process of restructuring of the hard currency deposits, which Russian enterprises held at Vnesheconombank of the former Soviet Union. Those deposits were frozen after a hard currency liquidity crisis in 1991 and subsequently replaced by five tranches of bearer U.S. dollar bonds at par. Reconciliation and allocation of Minfin Bonds was not finalized until the end of 1994 and a secondary market for these bonds was established only in 1995. The first two tranches were redeemed and two additional tranches were placed in 1996. As of the end 2005, there are four series of "Minfins" remaining on the market for the amount outstanding of US$7.66 billion. "Minfins" are Russian domestic securities and are subject to Russian law, including local tax laws.

Key Impediments to Development

Following several post-crisis years of limited domestic Federal bond market activity and development, in large part reflecting the improved federal budgetary position and improved external rating of Russia, there have recently been a number of developments that point towards a revitalisation of the Federal government domestic bond market. These are:

- Adoption of a debt strategy to increase reliance on domestic debt and to limit foreign currency issuance—as of end 2005 the ratios are: OFZ/(Eurobonds + "Minfins") = 4/5. Domestic Federal Debt/Foreign currency debt = 4/11.5.
- Increased reliance by the federal authorities on issuance of marketable securities on the domestic markets; discontinuation of the Central Bank purchases of government bonds in the primary market; proposed introduction of primary dealers and selected benchmark issues.
- Lengthening of the average maturity profile of the debt portfolio.

While the above steps may reasonably be expected to contribute to market development, key impediments remain:

- *Fragmented nature of the debt portfolio.* The Federal domestic debt portfolio is composed of both a large number of different types of instruments as well as a relatively large number of individual issues outstanding within each instrument category. This contrasts with recent trends in most OECD countries where government debt is increasingly composed of a relatively small number of more liquid benchmark bonds where the refinancing risk associated with a 'lumpier' maturity structure is managed in large part through market-based reverse auctions or switching programmes as the remaining maturity of older debt falls below a certain threshold.
- *Concentration of a significant portion of outstanding in 'buy-and-hold' portfolios.* The Central Bank, Sberbank, PFR, and GUK account for a majority of bond holdings, with the balance held by banks primarily for liquidity management as opposed to investment purposes. Non-bank participation in the market remains marginal, reflecting the limited yield/liquidity attractiveness of the sector as well as the limited development of the institutional savings sector in Russia to date.
- *Hybrid nature of instruments such as amortising bonds.* These hybrid instruments add a layer of complexity that, in an open market, would tend to result in lower demand in both the primary and secondary markets, translating into higher yields. Such instruments are not commonly used internationally. As noted above, with the increased international use of a smaller number of liquid benchmark issues, governments are increasingly relying on dynamic market based management of their refinancing risk through reverse auctions, switches, prefinancing, and so

forth. Several of these standard international market based practices are at present not possible in Russia or are significantly impeded by the detailed technical pre-scription of debt issuance ceiling in the legislation.

- *Absence of a straightforward, transparent and predictable primary issuance process containing well documented auction calendars and issuance plans.* While progress has been achieved in this area, the time period and detail covered by the Ministry's announcements falls short of what would normally be required by investors for planning purposes and what would normally be provided in OECD markets.
- *Absence of an effective primary dealership system to support both the primary and secondary markets.* While primary dealership systems do not constitute a "silver-bullet" solution to the structural weaknesses and market development impediments, inter-national experience has shown that an effective primary dealership framework can contribute significantly to the development of market depth and liquidity.
- *Absence of full open market pricing of primary market yields on federal bonds.* Given the impact of Sberbank dominant position and the nature of its special relationship with the government as issuer, the Federal government's foreign cur-rency borrowing activity and regulatory factors impacting the demand for fed-eral securities can mask the emergence of full open market pricing in both the primary and secondary markets. This can result in an expectation in the market that yields will be managed to lower levels than would otherwise be the case; and this coupled with the need for banks to hold government securities to manage their liquidity needs (through rediscounting with the Bank of Russia) and the limited issuance of Federal bonds because of its strong fiscal position and foreign debt issuance, has resulted in the emergence of a partially captive market with yields below what might otherwise pertain, curtailing investment interest by dis-cretionary (non-captive) investors. As a result, in a full open market environ-ment, secondary yields would tend to be higher than primary yields, giving rise to capital losses.
- *Very limited secondary market activity.* The market for government securities is quite illiquid, partially due to the issues raised above but also as a result of less than efficient institutional arrangements for the clearance and settlement of trades and the regulatory structure (see below). Specific obstacles in the regulatory framework include the prohibition of OTC trading, the missing legal basis for and standard-ization of the interbank repo transactions, and rules and regulations pertaining to the settlement requirements (such as the pre-depositing requirement)

In primary markets, auction procedures should be geared to maximum transparency, leaving as little scope to discretion as possible, as a means to encourage maximum auction participation. The following measures are likely to further the auctions' transparency with-out depriving MOF of requisite powers.

(i)   Auctions procedures should be embodied in a standing MOF regulation.
(ii) Auction calendars should be announced well in advance, preferably for the year as a whole. However, under exceptional circumstances the MOF should be able to conduct auctions with very short pre-announcement.

(iii) As the banks and other investors develop the capability to bid simultaneously on several issues, multiple auctions occurring on the same date should be held simultaneously, for both bidding and auction decision, following the standard international approach. This would provide MOF with more information to take its decisions and would expedite the auction procedures.

(iv) The authorities should continue to move towards allowing the market to set the cut-off rate, that is, for it to be set automatically on the basis of the bids. MOF should move away from setting the cut-off price on a discretionary basis and allocating an amount lower than the offered one; this should only be used to face a abnormal developments or violations of the auction rules, not to interfere with the evolution of yields. Full cancellation of an auction should be considered rarely, if at all, and restricted to very exceptional circumstances.

(v) Sberbank dominance in the auctions should be limited by introducing a limit on the bid(s) size from a single bidder.

(vi) A maximum amount for non-competitive bids should be set to strengthen price formation in the auction process. A minimum amount should be established for competitive bids to prevent the auction being distorted by irrelevant bids. An overall limit on the amount of non-competitive bids, such as 40 percent, should also be considered.

(vii) To broaden participation in the primary market, the authorities should encourage the widest possible group of investors to take part in the auction– financial and non-financial institutions, individuals, and foreigners. Anyone should be eligible to bid in the auction, although non-banks might be required, as in some countries, to bid through or with the guarantee of a bank.

(viii) After auction sales of additional securities by the MOF should be avoided. It vitiates the integrity of the auction mechanism and makes it more difficult for dealers to place securities obtained through the auction.

In the context of further developing the government securities market, the authorities may wish to consider setting up a market-making mechanism through a primary dealer (PD) system. A framework for designing a primary dealership system requires a realistic balance between the responsibilities and privileges of PDs in order both to ensure that they provide the required liquidity to the market and that the PD system is inherently commercially viable. Selection, ongoing monitoring and retention of individual PDs can be based on quantifiable and verifiable (via an inter-dealer broker or clearing house) performance relative to targets for individual PD primary market participation and secondary distribution. The integrity of the PD system can be protected by ongoing pre and post auction price analysis to guard against any collusion between one or more PDs.

Because of issues with the limited liquidity and concentrated investor base, Federal bonds in Russia do not constitute the anchor for the domestic currency yield curve that would be normal in most markets internationally. In Russia at present this role of reference point or benchmark for the pricing of borrowing by other issuers is largely played by the City of Moscow bonds. The development of the markets generally requires a reasonably liquid benchmark curve regardless of which issuer constitutes the benchmark. Nonetheless it is indicative of the limited depth of the Federal bond market in Russia that does not fill this role. Furthermore it may also reflect a perspective within the Ministry that, historically at least, did not attribute priority its role in promoting the development of the domestic federal and non-federal securities markets as an integral part of developing the financial infrastructure of the economy.

Key Priorities Going Forward

Key policy reform priorities for the development of the government bond market are as follows:

(i) Prepare Federal debt strategy including:
- objectives;
- projected funding plan;
- plans regarding consolidation of issues, reduction in number of issues, reverse auctions, switching, concentration of issuance in limited number of benchmarks, reopening, and so forth; and
- proposed full-year auction calendar and proposed arrangements re primary issuance process.

(ii) Establish and meet non-executive consultative industry working group regarding:
- primary dealer arrangements;
- primary issue process;
- benchmarks;
- OTC trading; and
- Repo transactions.

  Participation to be sought from authorities (CBR, MOF, MEDT, FSFM), legislative advice etc), infrastructure (MICEX, NDC, PARTAD etc) industry associations (banking associations, NFA, NAUFOR, etc) investment institutions as relevant.

(iii) Finalize and publish rules and modus operandi re primary dealership (PD), benchmarks and primary auction process, based on principle of maximum transparency and predictability:
- selection of primary dealers;
- agreement and documentation on privileges and obligations;
- capital adequacy requirements;
- ability to go short;
- access to repo;
- selection review process/term of appointment;
- performance review criteria, process and frequency of reviews of appointments (based on target shares of primary market issuance, volume and spread of investor distribution); and
- clear prohibition of collusion.

(iv) Streamline auction process:
- commitment to transparent and predictable annual calendar setting auction dates, amounts, maturities;
- more detailed quarterly/ weekly updates;
- limit cancellation to exceptional circumstances (to include cases of suspected collusion, based on analysis of pre-auction yield and spread analyses);

- use electronic platform;
- immediate feedback of auction results;
- limit non competitive auction;
- establish minimum bid level;
- limit allocation to single buyer (address additional investment needs of Sberbank through other types of issues); and
- gradually move towards market determination of cut-off (not immediate) when new process has taken root and adequate evidence of no collusion.

Sub-Sovereign Bond Market

Recent Evolution

Domestic Sub-Sovereign Bonds

The Russian subnational bond market consists of bonds issued by the Subjects of Federation (SF), and urban and municipal districts. SFs represent the second tier of the RF government and include all regions of Russia (republics, oblasts, territories, autonomous regions) as well as the City of Moscow and the City of St. Petersburg that have a special regional status. As of the end 2005, the Russian Federation is divided into 88 SFs. The third, municipal, level of the Russian federal system at the end of 2005 consisted of municipal districts. From January 1, 2006 the municipal level undergoes a reform, which is supposed to end by 2009, which leads to creation of one tier of municipal government in urban areas (urban districts) and two-tiered municipal government in the rural areas, consisting of municipal districts ("rayons") and settlements.

In the following, subjects of Federation, including Moscow and St. Petersburg, will be further referred to as "regions," and all governments of the municipal level will be referred to as "municipalities." Subsequently, bonds issued by the SFs (including cities of Moscow and St. Petersburg) will be referred to as "regional bonds," while bonds issued by various municipal governments will be referred to as "municipal bonds."

Most Russian subnationals can issue only domestic ruble denominated bonds. According to the current version of the RF Budget Code, Russian municipalities are prohibited from external borrowing, while Russian regions are allowed to borrow abroad only for the purpose of refinancing of the outstanding external debt. As of the end 2005, City of Moscow remained the only issuer of Russian subnational Eurobonds. For the purpose of this report, we are only looking into ruble denominated subnational bonds. In order to issue bonds, the regions and municipalities must receive a permission to do so from the federal Ministry of Finance (MOF).

Market Size and Structure (2002–05). Currently, the sub-sovereign market is the most rapidly growing segment of the domestic debt market. The number of regional bond issues and the size of regional debt are expected to grow further in the next few years due to large infrastructure investment needs and to the relatively low indebtedness of Russian regions.

The Russian sub-sovereign bond market first emerged in 1992 and grew substantially by 1998. The 1998 financial crisis had a devastating impact on the sub-sovereign bond market when a number of regions defaulted on their obligations and the market nearly seized to exist. St. Petersburg and Moscow were the only borrowers that continued to issue and service their debts through 1999–2000. Other issuers began to re-access the market only in late 2001, starting with Bashkortostan in November 2001 and followed by the Komi and Leningrad regions in December 2001.

The domestic subnational bond market has grown rapidly in the last four years both in terms of size and quality of issuance. The nominal value of bonds outstanding expanded from Rub23 billion by end 2001 to about Rub161 billion by end 2005, accounting for about 14 percent of the domestic bond market, by comparison to corporate bonds (28 percent) and government bonds (58 percent).

The number of issuers grew from just 5 regions at the end of 2001 to 31 regions and 15 municipalities (12 cities and 3 municipal districts) by end 2005. The number of publicly traded subnational bond issues increased at the same period from 58 to around 110. The issue size for regions (excluding Moscow, Moscow Oblast and St. Petersburg) grew from Rub200-500 million in 2001 to Rub1-3 billion in 2005. Moscow issues expanded to Rub5 billion. In April 2005, Moscow Oblast came up with the largest single bond issue of Rub12 billion.

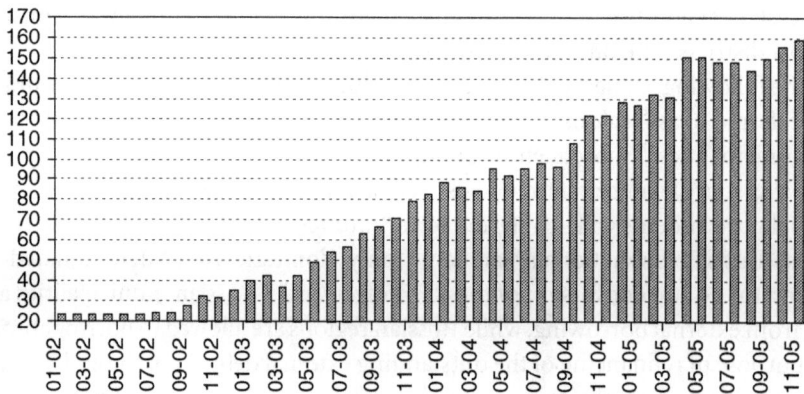

Figure 7. Subnational Bonds Outstanding, (nominal value as of End November 2005, billions of rubles)

Source: www.cbonds.ru.

Table 10. Market Structure as of End November, 2005

	Notional Out, billions of rubles	Number of Bonds	Number of Issuers
Moscow	61.4	14	1
Moscow Oblast	25.6	3	1
Saint Petersburg	8.2	12	1
Other regions	54.4	54	26
Municipalities	9.4	20	14
All Sub-sovereign Bonds	158.940	103	43

Source: Cbonds data, WB staff calculations.

As of the end November 2005, subnational bonds outstanding accounted for Rub158.9 billion. The market consisted of the 14 bonds issued by City of Moscow, 3 bonds issued by Moscow Oblast, 12 bonds issued by Saint Petersburg, 54 bonds issued by other 26 regions and 20 bonds issued by 14 municipalities.

The top three issuers, Moscow, Moscow Oblast, and St. Petersburg account for 60 percent of the market by nominal value. The remaining 40 percent of the bonds outstanding are divided among other regions (34 percent), and municipalities (6 percent).

Due to good credit fundamentals and effective debt management, Moscow issues have become the quasi-sovereign ruble bond benchmark on the Russian bond market. Most of Russian largest corporations are headquartered in Moscow and pay taxes to the local budget. In addition, the Moscow Financial Agency that is responsible for managing Moscow bonds has generated a well-developed yield curve across a range of maturities and established a market-maker system to ensure liquidity. Moscow papers vary from a few months to 10-year maturities and have the highest sub-sovereign ratings of BBB- (S&P) and Baa3 (Moody's).

In December 2005, two new regions and one new municipality as well as three existing issuers came up with new bond. The total number of issuing regions increased to 31 by end 2005.

Figure 8. Sub-sovereign Market Structure by Size, as of End November 2005

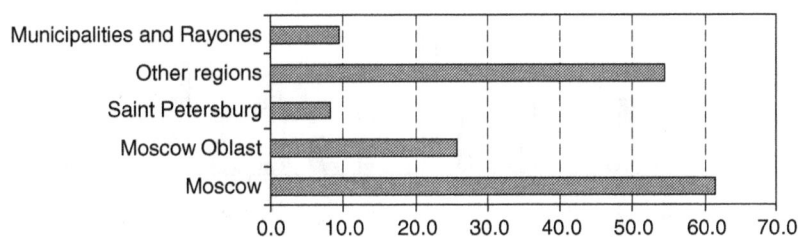

Source: Cbonds, WB staff calculations.

Table 11: Regional Bond Issues in December 2005

Date	Bonds	Placed, Nominal, Rub	% placed	Yield at Placement
12/01/2005	Tver Oblast-3	800 000 000		
12/05/2005	Komi Republic-8	1 000 000 000		
12/08/2005	Irkutsk Oblast-31002	900 000 000	100%	7.72%
12/20/2005	Novosibirsk Oblast-3401	2 500 000 000	100%	8.74%
12/22/2005	Kirov Oblast-34001	400 000 000	100%	8.66%
12/27/2005	Republic of Udmurtia-25001	1 000 000 000	100%	8.37%
12/28/2005	Yaroslavl Oblast-31005	374 350 000	74.87%	7.96%
12/29/2005	Yaroslavl Oblast-31005	470 000	0.37%	7.96%

Source: Rusbonds.ru.

Primary and Secondary Market (2002–05). Overall, new issuance has exceeded redemptions in the last four years. Most bonds have been placed through public auction MICEX, with few issues placed off exchange. Secondary trading in regional bonds is conducted primarily on MICEX and, to some extent over-the-counter (OTC). St. Petersburg and Karelia are two exceptions from the common rules, since these issuers have placed and traded their bonds only on St. Petersburg Interbank Currency Exchange (SPICEX). Some bonds have dual listing on both MICEX and SPICEX, but over 90 percent of their turnover accounts for MICEX.

Overall, the monthly turnover in subnational bonds has increased from less than Rub10 billion by end 2002 to over Rub80 billion by end 2005. The share of exchange turnover has always exceeded the OTC turnover varying from 60 to 80 percent.

Figure 9. Primary Market

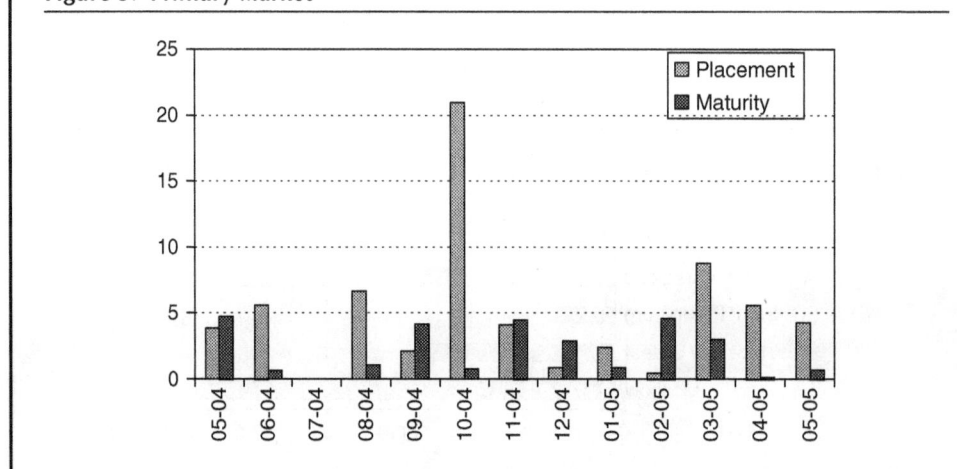

Source: Cbonds.

Figure 10. Turnover 2002–05

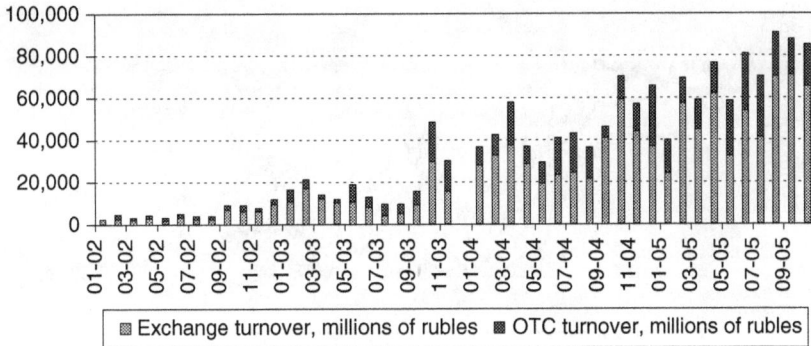

□ Exchange turnover, millions of rubles   ■ OTC turnover, millions of rubles

Source: www.cbonds.ru.

On average, Moscow and Moscow Oblast bonds account for over two-thirds of MICEX turnover. St. Petersburg bonds account for over 90 percent of SPICEX turnover in sub-sovereigns. The rest of the market is less liquid.

Sub-sovereign Bond Yields Dynamics (2002–05). The sub-sovereign yields declined rapidly in the last four years. Average annualized effective yields declined by about 4 percent in 2002, by another 5–6 percent in 2003, by 1 percent in 2004 and 1–1.5 percent in 2005. The issuance cost has declined to a very low level of less than 1 percent by end 2005, due to taxes and commission reduction, as well as tighter competition among underwriters. ZETBI-Muni index (one of the most comprehensive indicators for the average annualized effective yield of subnational bonds—calculated by Bank Zenit) has declined rapidly from 18–18.5 percent in the beginning of 2002 to 6.6–6.8 percent by end 2005. The Moscow (benchmark) annualized yield declined from 18 percent by end 2001 to around 5 percent by end 2005. The spreads of sub-sovereign to government bonds have narrowed substantially. In fact, due to higher than sovereign bonds liquidity, well development yield curve, and an investment-grade credit ratings that equals the sovereign credit rating for the Russian Federation, the City of Moscow bonds have become a well-recognized benchmark for both sub-sovereign and corporate ruble bonds. In 2005 Moscow bonds traded at nearly sovereign level of yield. The spreads of other sub-sovereign bonds to Moscow, have narrowed substantially as well, from up to 600 bps in 2002–2003 to up to 250 bps by end 2005.

In 2005 the Russian sub-sovereign market remained remarkably stable, although in 2003–04 there was significant volatility in the market. The factors that influenced price trends and volatility included change in ruble liquidity, foreign investor demand, change in the US interest rate expectations, as well as changes in perceived Russian political risks. Overall, sub-sovereign bonds yield dispersion has been lower than corporate bond yields dispersion.

The overall decline in yields was supported by raise of the sovereign credit ceiling, continuing appreciation of the national currency, high ruble liquidity, as well as real and perceived improvement in creditworthiness of the sub-sovereign issuers.

Figure 11. Sub-Sovereign Bond Yields 2002–05

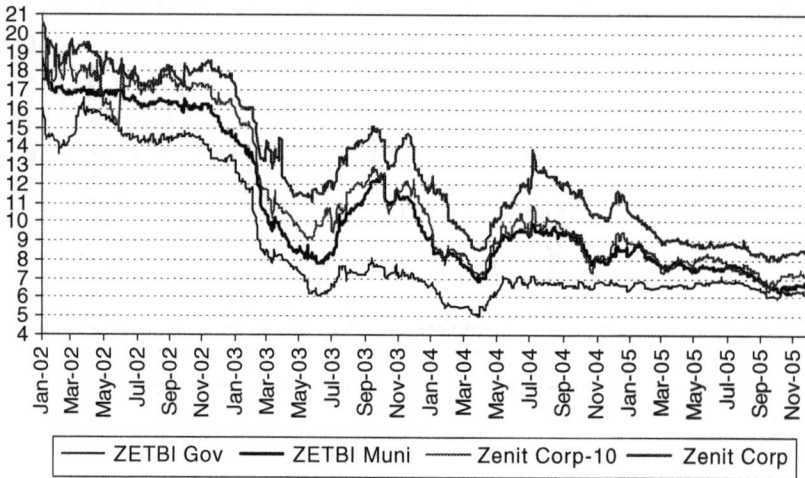

Source: Bank Zenit.

Market Inefficiency. As in many emerging markets, sound sub-sovereign bonds pricing has been hampered by high market concentration both in terms of size and turnover, market segmentation, low budget transparency of the second tier regions, and lack of adequate credit valuation. Liquidity and perceived credit quality are the two main factors in yields determination, while credit ratings do not yet play a major role in determination of yields and do not have precise effect on pricing. Issuers with one or two notch lower or higher rating can trade above the higher rated issues. Non-rated issues can price above rated issues as well.

Market Tiers. Overall sub-sovereign market can be divided into two or three tiers.

Tier 1 consists of the largest and most liquid issuers with long issuance history and highest credit quality. Currently this tier consists just of three regions: City of Moscow (S&P BBB, Rub61.4 billion, 14 bonds out, 39 percent of market size, turnover/outstanding > 25 percent); Moscow Oblast (Region) (S&P BB-, Rub25.6 billion, 3 bonds out, 16 percent of market size, turnover/outstanding >25 percent); City of St. Petersburg (S&P BB + , Rub8.2 billion, 12 bonds outs, 5 percent of the market, turnover/outstanding >25 percent).

Tier 2 consists of the regions and municipalities with previous history of bonds issuance (in the last three years), good or medium quality credit fundamentals. This tier includes most of the regions with bonds outstanding, which currently trade at spreads of 100–200 bps above Moscow.

Some analysts also identify in the market the Tier 3, consisting of the regional issues, particularly new ones, of marginal credit quality, and some municipal issues (financial situation of municipalities is generally more precarious than that of the regions). Prior to 2004, the third tier of the issuers was larger and more distinct, however, since 2004 the favorable development of the market, and real and perceived improvement in the subfederal issuers' creditworthiness have led to passing of many issuers from the third tier to the second one. Therefore in the report we will consider all the regions outside of the Tier 1 as belonging to the Tier 2.

According to estimates by leading market participants, commercial banks hold estimated 50–60 percent of all sub-sovereign issues. Investment banks and asset management companies are the next largest investors. The share of the non-state pension funds accounts for a few percents but is growing rapidly. The share of mutual funds and insurance companies remains marginal.

Foreign investors (who mostly have lower funding cost than local investors) have a strong impact on the pricing and liquidity of the issues. However, due to the low credit quality of the most of Russian issuers, foreign investors' interest is largely limited to the first tier issues, particularly in Moscow bonds, where foreigners hold up to 40 percent of bonds outstanding.

Sub-sovereign Eurobonds

The sub-sovereign Eurobond market is quite small, due to restrictions imposed by Budget Code, which states that Subjects of Russian Federation may only raise money abroad in order to refinance external debt. This prerequisite bares most Russian regions from Eurobond market. Municipalities are not allowed to borrow abroad at all. As of the end of 2005, only Moscow issues were outstanding on the market. The average annual yield declined from 9 percent in the beginning of 2002 to around 4–5 percent by the end of 2005.

Key Impediments to Development

In recent years, the authorities have taken a broad range of measures to strengthen the legal and regulatory framework for sub-sovereign borrowing with the objective to limit moral hazard.

First, the authorities have developed a comprehensive prudential framework for sub-sovereign borrowing under the Budget Code. The key elements of the framework are:
These limits are:

(1) *Debt outstanding limit*
   The maximum amount of a region's or municipality's debt cannot exceed the amount of revenues of their respective budget without taking into account the financial aid provided by other levels of government
(2) *Budget deficit limit*
   (i) The region's budget deficit cannot exceed 15 percent of the region's revenues without taking into account financial aid provided by the federal budget.
   (ii) The municipal budget deficit cannot exceed 10 percent of municipal budget revenues without taking into account the financial aid provided from budgets of other levels of government.
   Definition of budget deficit financing sources: bond issues, loans, budget loans and budget credits from other levels, proceeds of sub-sovereign asset sales, changes in balances on accounts.

(3) *Current expenditure limit*
Current expenditures of a regional or municipal budget cannot exceed the revenues of the respective budget.
(4) *Debt service limit*
The maximum amount of debt service cannot exceed 15 percent of revenues of a regional or municipal budget.

Additional restrictions are:

▨ Guarantee limit, set at 5 percent of expenditures of sub-sovereign entities.
▨ Limitation of foreign borrowing to refinancing of existing foreign debt by SFs, and prohibition of foreign borrowing by municipalities.

Second, the authorities have adopted measures to deal with cases of debt default by a sub-sovereign entity, namely Budget Code provisions allowing higher levels of the Federal system to intervene and take control of budget execution by lower levels in case of breach of prudential regulations on sub-sovereign borrowing or in case of failure to repay debt obligations.

Thirds, the authorities have adopted detailed procedures for the registration of sub-sovereign securities by the Ministry of Finance, and for the listing of these securities on the stock exchange (MICEX). These procedures allow MOF to ensure that entities issuing securities on the market respect rules and regulations concerning budget execution and prudential framework, and appropriate disclosure for investors.

Despite these considerable advances, the risk of moral hazard remains present on the sub-sovereign finance market, mainly due to difficulties in the implementation the prudential framework for sub-sovereign borrowing.

First, about 20 out of 88 SFs have broken the budget deficit limit at least one year over the 2000–02 period. In addition, about 8 SFs have broken the debt exposure limit set by the Budget Code. The overexposure of these SFs is even higher if one takes into account the amount of accounts payable by SFs both with respect to mandated expenditures and with respect to civil contracts. In practice, that in itself may underestimate their real exposure, since there is a tendency by SFs to underreport accounts payable.

Second, at the SF level, budget loans represented 12 to 15 percent of budget deficits over the 2000–02 period. The repayment of budget loans by SFs has gone down dramatically over the past three years. While in 2000, repayments of budget loans by SFs exceeded the amount borrowed in that year, the repayment ratio felt to 71 percent in 2001 and to 51 percent in 2002. As a result, budget loans, which are established to cover short-term liquidity gaps only, are becoming an instrument to finance structural deficits by SFs. At the municipal level, dependency on budget loans to finance deficits is significantly higher than at the SF level, ranging from 45 to 54 percent over the 2000–02 periods.

Third, there is no available data on the level of guarantees made by sub-sovereign entities to third parties, making control of the prudential limit on guarantees by sub-sovereigns impossible to enforce.

Fourth, sub-sovereign entities are in some cases shareholders of regional banks that make loans to them, often on favorable terms, significantly raising moral hazard.

Finally, the framework for intervention by higher levels in the Federal system in case of debt default by a sub-sovereign entity remains vague. The procedures applying to sub-sovereign debt default remain far behind those in place in the case of corporate bankruptcy. In addition, the Budget Code does not regulate the procedural issues of transfer of budget management responsibility to a different level of the Federal system in case of sub-sovereign default.

Key Priorities Going Forward

Key policy reform priorities for the development of the sub-sovereign bond market are as follows:

   (i) Enforce prudential limits by denying approvals for bond issuance for SFs and municipalities in breach of these limits.

  (ii) Include past due payments in calculation of indebtedness limits.

 (iii) Enforce repayment of existing budget loans and other Federal debts within the fiscal year.

 (iv) Eliminate new related party borrowing from affiliated banks, and adopt standards for competitive selection for bank creditors and bond underwriters.

  (v) Adopt law on bankruptcy of regions and municipalities, substituting for current provisions on sub-sovereign debt default in the Budget Code.

Corporate Bond Market

Recent Evolution

Domestic Corporate Bonds

Emerging in 2000 as real financing option, the corporate bond market is the most dynamically developing segment of the domestic bond market. From the end of 2000 to the end of 2005 nominal amount of corporate bonds outstanding increased from Rub39 billion (US$1.4 billion) to Rub481 billion (US$16.7 billion). In relative terms, bonds outstanding grew from 0.5 percent of GDP by end 2000 to 2.2 percent of GDP by end 2005.

In nominal terms, the market has expanded most rapidly in the last two years, growing on average by Rub9 billion per month in 2004 and by Rub15 billion in the first 10 month of 2005. Corporate bond issuance has far outstripped the redemption volumes. The average size of corporate bond issue has expanded from around Rub500 million in 2000 to Rub5 billion in 2005. The average duration increased from less than one year in 2000–01 to three years in 2005. The average yields to maturity for one-year issue declined from over 20 percent in December 2001 to 8 percent by end 2005, with real yields have turned negative since the beginning of 2003. By the end 2005, corporate market was comprised of over 310 bonds issued by over 220 companies. Over 80 percent of the outstanding volume was placed by the non-financial corporations and less than 20 percent was placed by banks and other financial institutions.

Ruble denominated corporate bonds did not exist in any form prior to 1998 crisis, since the mushrooming GKO market would have essentially crowded out any perspective corporate issue. The first securities issued as ruble corporate bonds appeared on the market in the 1999, but these securities were not used as a financing instrument, but rather as a financial mechanism of repatriation for foreign investor's rubles trapped in S-account

Figure 12. Corporate Bonds Market Dynamics

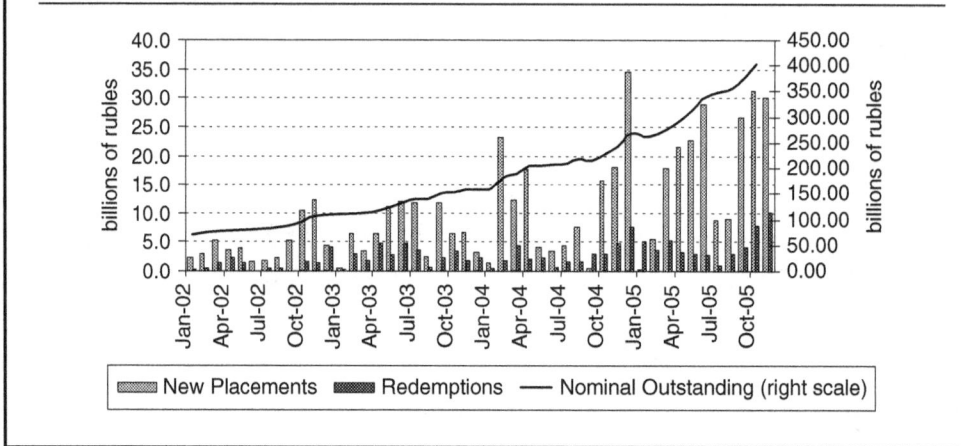

Source: Cbonds.

after the GKO default in August 1998. Foreign investors could buy these pseudo-bonds for Rubles in S-accounts and get dollars from issuer in exchange. The economic sense for the issuer of this "pseudo-bonds" was the off-market US$/Rub exchange rate used in the transactions, which allowed issuer to purchase cheap ruble from the foreign investors. The economic sense for the investor was to repatriate their funds trapped in ruble accounts. Although around US$1 billion of the "pseudo-bonds" were issued, no actual borrowing by the issuers took place. By the time the Central Bank eased restrictions on "S-accounts" in late 2001, most "S-account" money had already left the country.

In the first years following the 1998 crisis, most capital investments were financed from the retained earnings. But with increasing capital needs this strategy reached the limits. Thus, many large domestic corporations turned to capital markets to fund their capital investments needs, first through issue of veksels, then through bond issuance. The first real corporate bonds, issued as traditional financing mechanism begin to appear on the market in mid-2000 to early 2001. Large blue chip corporations primarily in oil & gas industry as well as major banks were the first to utilize the new financing option on the ruble debt market. As of the end 2001, oil and gas companies, as well as major banks accounted for 60 percent of the bonds outstanding. TNK was the first blue chip company to issued regular bond in early 2001. Gazprom, UES and Russian Aluminum followed the lead and by 2002, bonds become an important financing instrument for the large blue chip companies.

In 2000–02, corporate bond market did not have set standards for bond terms, valuation methods and benchmarks. Issue sizes ranged from Rub100 million to Rub3 billion. Only a few blue-chip issues were traded, while the rest of the bonds did not have liquid secondary market. Official bond maturities ranged from one to three years, but, since the market was not ready to absorb any paper with maturity greater than one year, most issuers offered binding buy-back option or so-called "Offerta," which reduced effective duration of bonds to less than one year. "Offerta" in most cases was equivalent to put option, provided every quarter, or every six months or once a year. Larger issuer provided put option on annual basis, while smaller issuers provided a put option quarterly or semi-annually. In some cases set strikes for put options were provided for the whole life of the bond, but in most cases, only the next put strike was known, while the next put strike and its timing where announced prior to the previous put maturity. With effective duration of the most of the issues less than one year, corporate bonds were essentially a short-term debt instruments competing with bank loans. Because bond structure was not standardized and, in many cases exotic, the effective yield to maturity was difficult to calculate. No clear benchmark existed for bonds prior to the end of 2002. Corporate securities where compared to GKO/OFZ curve which was not the most appropriate benchmark for the market, due to peculiar investor's base of the government bond market. Market was dominated by banks, which used bonds as an instrument to place short-term liquidity. Thus, there was no stable demand in the market.

In 2003–04, the bond market became more standardized and mature. Issuers begin to place larger bonds of set sizes of Rub500 million, 1 billion, 3 billion, and so forth. Issues smaller than Rub500 million become not attractive for investors and mostly illiquid. More bonds were issued with fixed coupon rate and fewer put options. Issuers provided put strikes for the whole life of the bond with less put frequency. Time-to-put extended from six month to one year, then to eighteen month. Taking advantage of favorable market conditions of 2003, Gazprom placed the Rub10 billion issue with three years to maturity without a put option (a largest bond issue at that time). In 2004, most bonds were issued without a put option for average time to maturity of three years. By end 2005, the average duration of corporate issues was about three years.

Starting from 2003, bonds issued by the city of Moscow become the most liquid papers on the non-government bond market. With high liquidity and variety of standardized issues of various maturities, Moscow bond begin to play a role of the benchmark on the domestic non-government bond market, which includes both corporate and sub-sovereign bonds. Corporate issue began to be evaluated based on the spread to Moscow yield curve. In 2005, some investment banks (Troika Dialog) offered an improved benchmark—Moscow zero-coupon yield curve.

Right from the emergence of the corporate bond segment, most corporate issues have been placed on MICEX through issuance of global paper certificate with storage of the global certificate in the National Depositary Center. This form of issuance has been successfully used by Russian government in the placement of GKO/OFZ. Corporate issues quickly realized the effectiveness of the system and this form of issuance has been used by most market participants. A few issues were placed on RTS and St. Petersburg Currency Exchange, but 99 percent of issues were placed on MICEX.

Secondary trading is conducted primarily on MICEX and OTC. RTS and St. Petersburg Currency Exchange tried to organize exchange trading in corporate bonds, but failed to attract much investor's interest. Today nearly 100 percent of exchange trading in corporate bonds is conducted on MICEX and settled through the NDC. OTC trading accounts for 40–60 percent of the total turnover, depending on the market conditions. In the volatile market, trading shifts OTC. Average monthly turnover on secondary market for corporate bonds on MICEX grew from Rub0.5 billion in 2000 to Rub75 billion in 2005.

Figure 13. Corproate Bonds Turnover

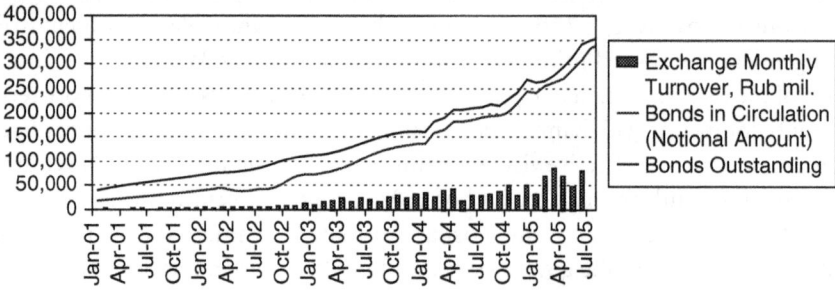

Legend:
- Exchange Monthly Turnover, Rub mil.
- Bonds in Circulation (Notional Amount)
- Bonds Outstanding

Source: Cbonds.

The supply of corporate bonds and diversification of the issuer base improved with overall economic growth and development of Russian corporate sector. The first major debt issues came from blue chip companies in banking, electricity, and oil & gas sector, followed by metallurgy and others. In 2001, oil & gas and banking sector accounted for over 50 percent of the bonds issuance. In 2002, companies from metallurgy, mining, and machine building industry tapped into the ruble debt market. In 2003, companies from telecommunication and food industries also become active issuers. Meanwhile, major blue chip companies in oil & gas, electricity, and banking expanded their borrowing program through Eurobonds and Credit Linked Notes (CLNs) which offered better terms than ruble market at that time.

The demand for corporate bonds (investor base) is becoming more stable, although commercial banks still dominate. The role of institutional investors has grown significantly,

Figure 14. Corporate Bonds, Types of Issuers

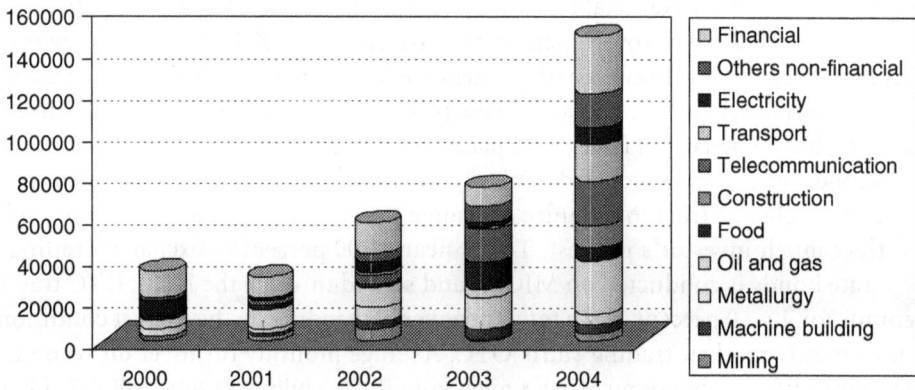

Legend:
- Financial
- Others non-financial
- Electricity
- Transport
- Telecommunication
- Construction
- Food
- Oil and gas
- Metallurgy
- Machine building
- Mining

Source: MICEX and WB Staff calculations.

Figure 15. Investor Base (percentages)

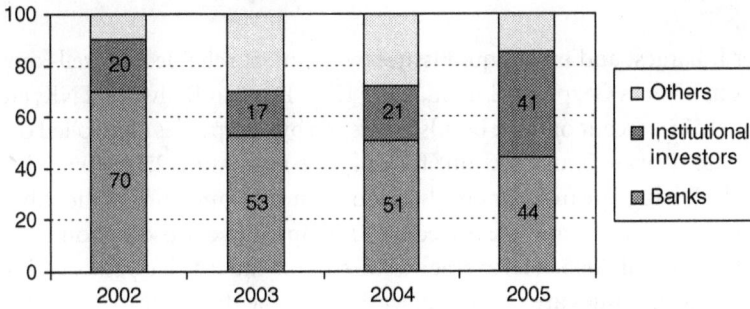

Source: Troika Dialog Estimates.

especially in 2004–2005. According to Troika Dialog estimates, the share of banks in corporate bond market has decline from 70 percent in 2002 to 44 percent by mid 2005. The main
investors in the banking sector are Sberbank, alone accounting for 9 percent of the market,
and handful of other large state-controlled banks accounting for the major portion of
banks' share. At the same time, the share of institutional investors, which includes insurance firms, non-state pension funds, investment funds, and asset management companies
investing on behalf of the other three types of institutional investors, increased from around
20 to 41 percent with insurance firms accounting for 18 percent, non-state pension funds
for 15 percent, investment funds for only 3 percent and asset management companies for
5 percent. The role of insurance firms and non-state pension funds developed most promi-
nently. Starting from 2004 and especially in 2005, the non-resident investors were quite
active on the market, with their share increasing to 11 percent as of mid 2005. The activity
of foreign investors is expected to increase significantly with currency liberalization set for
the beginning of 2007.

Figure 16. Investor Base as of 2005

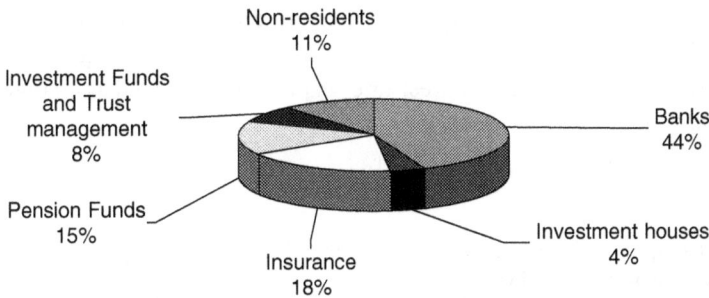

Source: Troika Dialog.

Credit quality and issue size are the main conditions effecting the yields and tenor of the new placements. According to these two criteria, corporate bonds can be broken down into three tiers:

- Tier I: Largest and most liquid issues by the most reliable and well-known corporations such as Gazprom, Lukoil, RAO UES, Russian Railways, TNK, etc. Approximately 75 percent of these bonds are issued by companies controlled or supported by state. Private issues account for only the remaining 25 percent. According to Troika Dialog, the first tier bonds account for over one third of the ruble corporate bonds outstanding and are priced 0 to 120 bps above Moscow bonds as of the second quarter of 2005. The average issue size for the fist tier bonds is about Rub3-5 billion. Most issues are rated by at least one of the three global rating agencies with global scale rating equivalent to BB- to BBB- by S&P scale.
- Tier II: Large and medium notional size issues (fairly liquid), of good credit quality or medium and small issues of the best credit quality Russian corporates—Central Telecom, Mechel Steel Group, Ural Svyaz Invest, Pyaterochka, Severstal-Avto, Vyksa Steel Works, TMK, Megafon, UN Interbrew, and so forth. According to Troika Dialog, the second tier corporates account for slightly less the one third of the market. According to Troika calculations, the second tier bonds are priced at 120–330 bps above Moscow. Majority of issues are rated at the rate equivalent to B – to BB+ on the S&P global scale; however, some issues do not have rating at all.
- Tier III: illiquid (small) issues of reasonable or poor credit quality—Nidan, PIT, Tinkoff, JFC, SU-155, and so forth. Most issuers are not rated and do not have financial statements in international standards. Spreads for this are around 400 bps and above Moscow bonds.

Growing excess liquidity with lowering inflation in the Russian economy in 2002–04 translated in a rapid decline in yields, a compression of spreads and a lengthening of maturities on the domestic corporate bond market. Average corporate yields for the top 10 corporate bonds (first tier) declined from average 18 percent in January of 2002 to average 16 percent in December 2002 to average 11 percent in December 2003 to average 9 percent in December 2004 and to average 7 percent in November 2005[5]. Spreads of the second tier and third tier bonds to the first tier bonds have narrowed from up 10 percent in 2002–2003 to 4 percent in November 2005.

At present corporate yields are still very volatile. In the last three years, the market went through three full price cycles, with yields fluctuating by +/–400 bps on average. The factors that influenced price trends and volatility included changes in ruble liquidity, foreign investors demand, U.S. interest rates expectations as well as changes in Russian political risk.

---

5. Yields description is based on the series of bond indices calculated by Bank Zenit. This seems to be one of the most accurate and convenient indicators of bonds yields. Bank Zenit calculates yields indices for the portfolio of the main government bonds, municipal bonds, top 10 corporate bonds, and portfolio of the most 1st and 2nd tier corporate bonds. All yield indices are calculated with the start date of January 1, 2002.

Figure 17. Corporate Bond Average Annualized Yields 2002–05

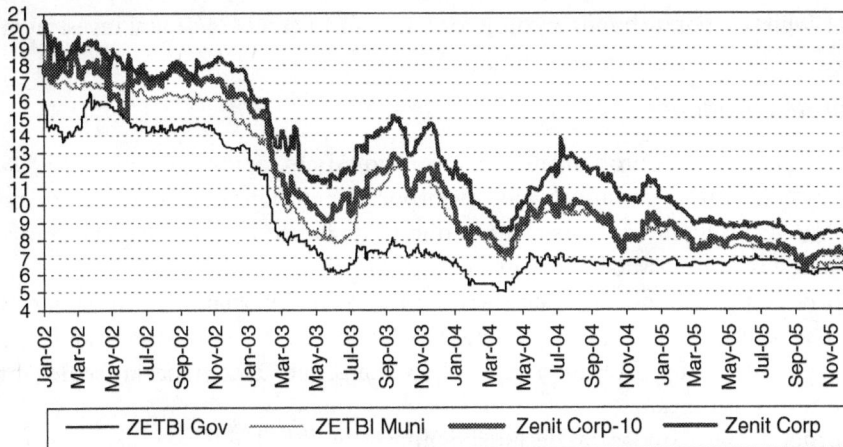

Source: Cbonds.

Investments into corporate bonds are taxed at 13 percent for individual and 24 percent for corporates. Considering the inflation rate and bonds taxation, real term yields for the first tier bonds turned negative in 2003. The yields for the second tier bonds become negative in 2004–05. Currently, only third tier bonds could yield positive return in real terms.

Starting from 2004, corporate bonds issuance becomes competitive with bank lending. By the beginning of 2005, rates on primary offerings were within 10–12 percent and for the large blue chip companies 7–8 percent (without accounting for bond servicing fee of 1–1.5 percent), in compare with long-term ruble loan rates of 10–14 percent. In 2005, corporate bonds become cheaper than bank loans.

Figure 18. Corporate Yields Dynamics

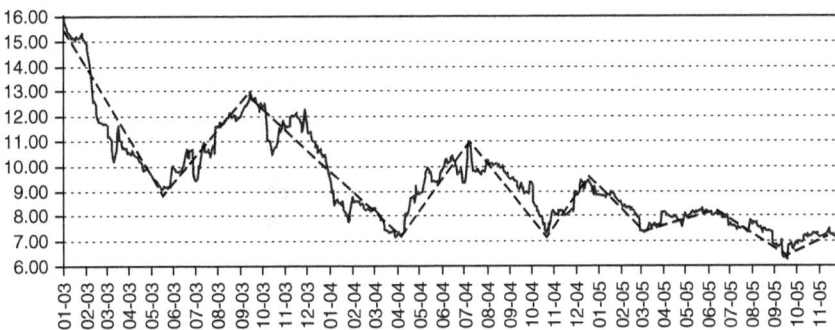

Source: Troika Dialog.

One remaining problem is that bond issuance proceed often time go for financing of the current needs rather than capital investments. According to CBR Banking Supervision 2004 report, bank loans account for 6.3 percent of the financing of fixed capital investment in 2004, while corporate bonds account for less than 1 percent of capital investments.)

Corporate Eurobonds

The Russian corporate Eurobond market is very liquid and rapidly growing. From US$2.03 billion by end 2001, the nominal value of corporate Eurobonds outstanding expanded to about US$40.5 billion (55–60 percent of bonds are issued by non-financial companies, with the rest of bonds issued by financial institutions).

Corporate Eurobonds are underwritten by major international investment house (Deutsche Banks, ING Bank, JP Morgan, Merrill Lynch, UBS, and so forth) and traded on London Stock Exchange, Luxembourg Stock Exchange and OTC Trades are settled through Euroclear or Clearstream.

Corporate Eurobond yields declined significantly in the last three years. From the level of 11–13 percent by end of 2001 to 5.5–7.5 percent by end 2005. The bonds of companies related to state are traded at 0 to 150 bps spread to Russian sovereign Eurobonds. Other corporate bonds are mostly traded at spread of over 100 bps to Russian sovereign Eurobonds.

Key Impediments to Development

The overheating of the domestic bond market raises both a macroeconomic risk and a market risk. The macroeconomic risk arises principally from the possible impact of a drop in the price of oil on domestic liquidity and on interest rates. The market risk arises from the increasing disconnect between corporate bond yields and the riskiness of specific issues, and from the possible impact of a corporate bond default on the risk perception of investors.

The Government is taking several measures to deal with corporate market risk. These measures are specifically aimed at improving disclosure and strengthening standards of corporate governance for listed companies.

The Government is taking several measures to increase the extent and quality of disclosure by corporations listed on exchanges.

First, the Government is encouraging listed corporations to improve their accounting standards through the adoption of IAS. Already, over 40 largest corporations that are trading on foreign stock exchanges have adopted IAS or US GAAP. However, smaller companies face both constraints and a lack of incentives to move to IAS. First, most of them lack qualified staff, and do not have access to a translation of IAS in Russian. Second, the absence of risk pricing on the domestic bond market may act as a disincentive for smaller companies to improve their current accounting practices. These realities have led the Government to push back the deadline for the general adoption of IAS by listed corporations beyond the original target date of January 2004.

Second, the Government is taking steps to improve the governance of listed corporations. On April 4, 2002, the FCSM issued a regulatory note on "Recommendations on the Application of the Corporate Governance Code." The Code, prepared by the Russian

Institute of Directors at the request of FCSM, is based on internationally recognized governance principles developed by the OECD. The Code sets out detailed recommendations on the principles of corporate governance for all corporate entities, most importantly for joint stock companies seeking access to capital markets. It covers standards for general shareholders meetings, companies Board, companies' executive bodies, corporate secretary, major corporate actions, corporate information disclosure, supervision of financial and business operations of the company, dividends, and resolution of corporate conflicts.

Following up on the issuance of the FCSM regulatory note, MICEX and RTS inserted differential corporate governance requirements in their respective listing categories. Regarding MICEX, listing in the A1 category requires firms to respect the Corporate Governance Code. However, as there are no formal criteria to verify compliance with the provisions of the Code, to date this requirement is based on self-declaration. FCSM is currently developing a set of criteria in collaboration with the exchanges. Once these criteria are adopted, FCSM plans to use them as a basis for assessing compliance of listed companies with the provisions of the Code.

At the micro level, recent policy changes include the reduction in registration tax from 0.8 to 0.2 percent, with the introduction of a cap on the tax of some US$3000 equivalent. This has contributed to an increased use of corporate bonds generally, and also relative to financial veksels in particular as a source of working capital finance; apart from earlier limitations on the availability of term funding beyond one year, the previous higher rate of registration tax was a significant factor behind the issuance of bonds with put options (offertas), as well as the earlier growth of veksel financing. While still larger in terms of outstanding, the market for veksels now appears to be declining and that of corporate bonds growing.[6] It appears desirable to encourage an "approved" market in commercial paper to develop to meet corporate' short term working capital finance needs. For this market to be cost effective, registration could be exempted for companies with an A1/A2 listing on MICEX (or equivalent), trading could be OTC and, to protect retail investors, issue amounts could be restricted to wholesale levels (e.g. Rouble 3 million plus).

Key Priorities Going Forward

Building on these efforts, the authorities could consider taking a number of measures that would strengthen the foundations of the corporate bond market, through improving market transparency and the quality of corporate governance. In particular, the authorities could consider:

(i)   adopting a realistic calendar for the issuance of new listing rules requiring corporations to adopt IAS as a condition for listing on MICEX and RTS (first tier), and enforcing its implementation;

(ii) requiring listed companies to disclose their ultimate controllers (i.e. ultimate economic beneficiaries), as is customarily the case on major OECD exchanges; and

(iii) adopting a set of Corporate Governance Code criteria and proceeding with their enforcement by FCSM.

---

6. In particular it is understood that Gazprom has indicated it is discontinuing the issuance of veksels.

Equity Markets

Recent Evolution

Russian equity market capitalization expanded rapidly in the last five years from Rub1.2 trillion (US$41 billion) by end 2000 to Rub6.9 trillion (US$247.5 billion) by end 2004 and to about Rub15 trillion (over US$500 billion) by end 2005. In relation to GDP, the market grew from 17 percent of GDP by end 2000 to 41 percent of GDP by end 2004, and estimated 70 percent of GDP level by end 2005. In relative terms the market grew at the rate far exceeding GDP growth, with the exception of 2004, when market capitalization in relation to GDP declined from 44 to 41 percent, due to downfall in market prices, particularly related to YUKOS affair. In 2005, new companies admitted for trading as a result of energy sector reforms along with the surge in price of blue chips (primarily Gazprom) led to unprecedented growth more than doubling market capitalization in nominal terms and increasing it from 40 to 60 percent of GDP level in relative terms.

RTS Index grew by 90 percent in 2001, 48 percent in 2002, 46 percent in 2003, only 1 percent in 2004 and 93 percent in 2005 in ruble terms. The equity prices grew rapidly in 2001–03 due to favorable macroeconomic situation in Russia and growing ruble liquidity. Due to Yukos affair in 2003–04, the market plunged in the first half 2004, but grow at the year end to extremely favorable macroeconomic conditions for Russia (high oil and gas prices, U.S. dollar depreciation against all major currencies, high ruble liquidity), as well as perceived and real increase in sovereign credit quality (increase in ratings to investible grade by major rating agencies).

Prior to 2005, capitalization expanded rapidly mostly due to the price appreciation of the outstanding first and second tier companies. However in 2005, capitalization expanded not only due to the price appreciation, but also due to the increase in the number of stocks

Figure 19. Corporate Bonds Outstanding

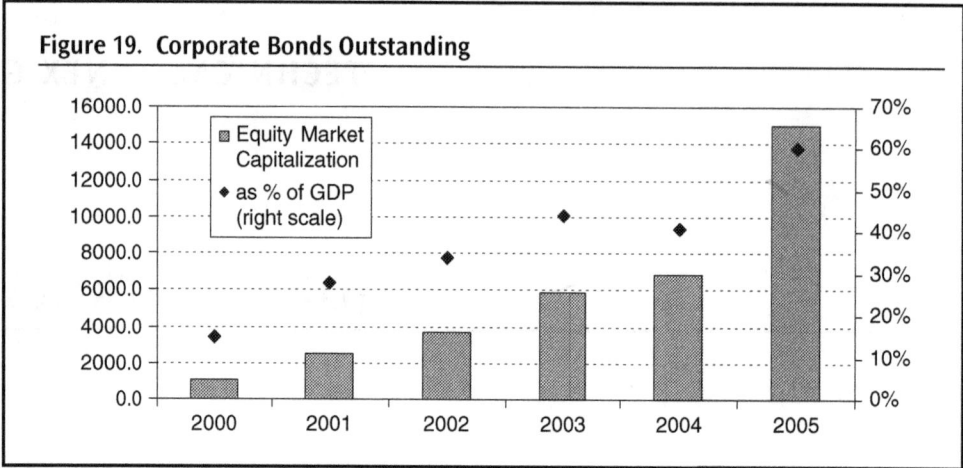

Source: Cbonds and WB staff calculations.

admitted for trading from 215 at end 2004 to 277 by end 2005. The list of new liquid stock (added through domestic IPO) include military jet producer IRKUT, cosmetics company Kalina, food retailer Sedmoi Continent. Securities actively traded in London, included new additions, AFK Systema, Novatek, NLMK.

Currently, Russian equity market is one of the largest in Eastern Europe with over 270 stocks admitted for trading on major domestic exchanges and market capitalization of estimated 70 percent of GDP level by end 2005. As observed in many emerging markets, trading activity is limited and concentrated in a few blue chip stocks. Comparing to other markets, liquidity is lower than observed in the equity markets of Korea, Turkey, Taiwan, or Thailand.

Despite rapid growth in capitalization (75 percent average nominal growth for the 2000–05 period), the market is highly concentrated in terms of size and trading activity among a dozen of issuers, mostly in the oil & gas, electricity, metals and telecom industry.

Figure 20. Evolution of the Russian Equity Market (1996–2005)

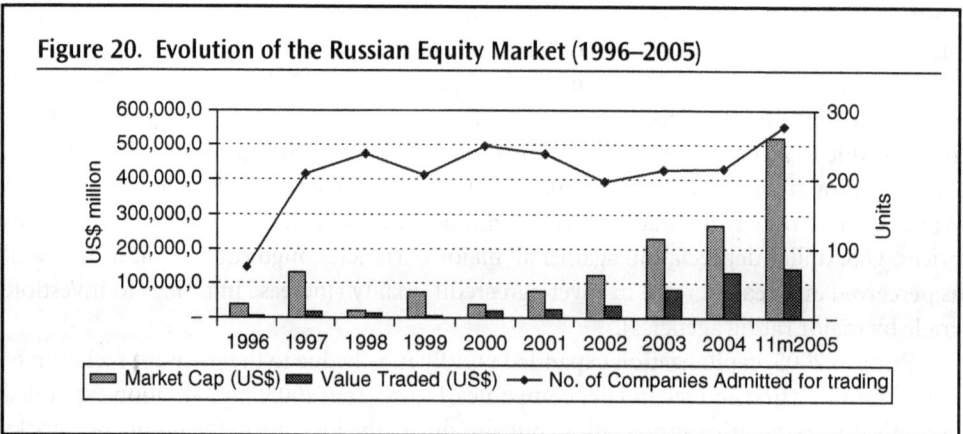

Source: EMDB.

In 2004, top 10 blue chip companies accounted for 78 percent of the total market capital-ization. In 2005, the top 10 blue chip companies accounted for 76 percent of the total mar-ket capitalization. Gazprom alone accounts for over one-third of the market capitalization by end 2005 (more in January 2006).

High market concentration is partly due to the low level of new issuances and the lim-ited number of shares in free circulation (free float). As a result of privatization, a large number of joint stock companies were created, generating over 200 stocks admitted for trading by 2000. However, based on limited available data, as of 2004–2005 market free float[7] remains very low, estimated at 5–25 percent for different companies, effectively decreasing the size of the readily investible market. According to a recent CSFB report,[8] the Russian equity market has the lowest average free float among the 26 countries in the MSCI Index at about 23 percent (in the index). It is also estimated by the market participants that banks hold about half of the traded shares.

Domestic IPO are becoming a reality, although the volume of Russian companies' issuance abroad is far exceeding domestic IPOs. Starting from the first quasi IPO in 2002 (Apteka 36.6), Russian companies begin to tap the domestic equity market (one issue in 2003, five issues in 2004, and three issues in 2005). More issues are in the pipeline for 2006.

At the same time Russian companies increase equity issuance abroad through ADR programs in New York and GDR programs in London. Additionally, a number of Russian companies access LSE market through listing of foreign companies with major control over Russian assets (Foreign SPV or Russian offshore companies). In 2005, there was wave of new IPOs through ADRs, GDRs, and SPVs, primarily in London, a number of companies from various industry have placed additional shares in London. The main problem here is that Russian companies do not use domestic market enough to attract new capital. Specif-ically a problem is the issue of foreign SPV on Russian companies. This shares cannot be

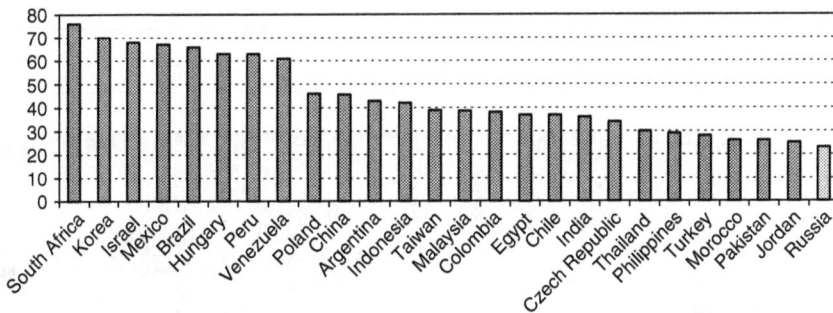

Figure 21. Weighted Average Free Float for Emerging Market Equities

Source: CSFB, MSCI.

---

7. Free float ratio represents the percentage of total share capital of the companies that are offered to the public, i.e. not held by owners.

8. Russian Equity Strategy, CSFB, March 2004.

Table 12: Domestic IPOs

	1996	1997	1998	1999	2000	2001	2002	2003	2004	2005	percent of 2005
Domestic IPOs							13.3			223	5%
International IPOs (ADR and GDR)	111	104	–	–	323	0	146	–	233	2 487	60%
International IPOs (SPV)							15.6	66.2	73.4	1434.25	35%
SPO		33.6	0	55.80	187	0	12.6	53.8	1931	0	0%

Source: CCMD and WB Staff calculations.

traded in Russia, thus this securities will not be traded in Russia. Outsourcing investment banking, trading to London.

Current situation is that Russian large and mid-size companies do not view domestic market as a source of new funds preferring raising equity capital through ADR, GDR and SPV issuance in London and New York. In 2005, Russian companies raised US$2487 billion through ADRs and GDRs, US$1434 billion through foreign parent companies or SPVs, in compare with only US$223 million raised on the domestic market. Overall in 2005, nearly 95 percent of equity capital was raised by Russian companies abroad, while only about 5 percent was raised through domestic IPOs.

Due to undercapitalized trading and settlement infrastructure secondary trading in Russian equities began to shift to international markets in 2003–04, causing a major concern for domestic market institutions and the market regulator. The turnover of Russian depository receipts in LSE, Deutsche Burse, and NYSE become greater than domestic trading on MICEX and RTS combined since the last quarter of 2003. This

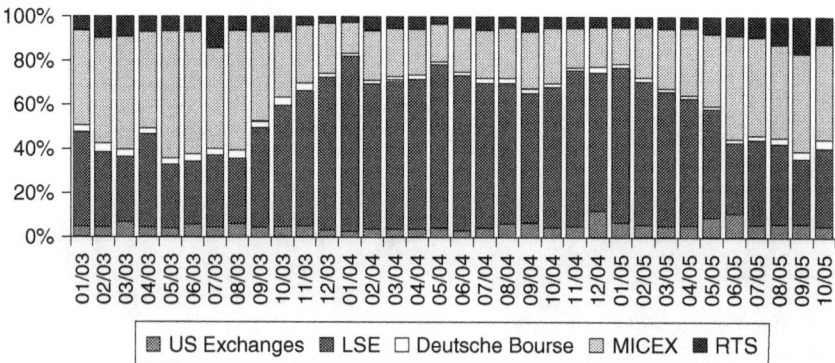

Figure 22. Russian Equities Turnover 2003–04

Source: FSFM.

Figure 23. RTS Index Performance

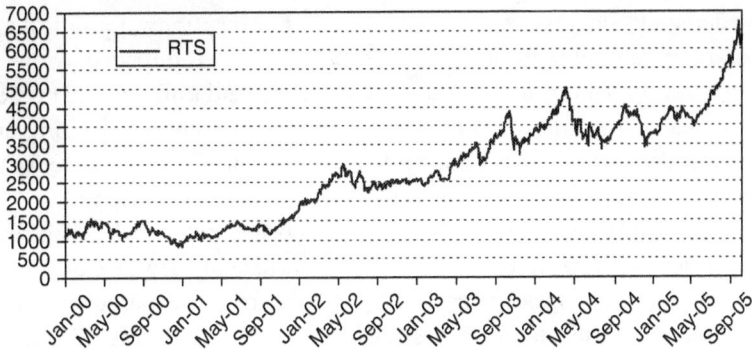

problem become less acute in 2005, when due to high ruble liquidity and lack of available Russian instruments on international markets, have shifted liquidity back to domestic market with MICEX and RTS accounting for about 60 percent of the total Russian equity turnover by end 2005.

Russia was among the top performing emerging markets in 1999 to mid-2003. In the second half 2003–04, the equity market moved up and down, primarily due to the uncertainties surrounding the future of Yukos and concern about the future of a few other blue chip issuers, primarily in gas, oil and energy sectors. Recent instability in the market is a further illustration of the sectoral concentration of the Russian equity market. In 2005, the market grew rapidly due to high oil prices, rapid price appreciation of Gazprom (due to increase in gas prices and preparations for liberalization of Gazprom trading), high ruble liquidity.

Key Impediments to Development

On the supply side, the development of the equity market is hampered by a corporate preference towards owner control within a small closed group, and a general reluctance to operate companies as publicly traded entities with a large diverse group of shareholders. In this context, financial industrial groups (FIGs) tend to favor diversification through acquiring control of companies and integrating them in the group rather than through holding of diversified portfolios of traded securities. The free float of many Russian companies remains extremely low from 5 to 25 percent. The heavy concentration of the market in a few large companies constitutes another impediment to market development, as medium-size companies may feel too small to access the market place on their own. This may be reinforced by the fear of hostile takeovers. The large companies if decide to go to IPO market, prefer to raise funds abroad. Mid and small companies are not ready for domestic IPO. Potential IPO candidates are either too big to feel the need for an IPO or too small to feel it possible. There could be a case for building market facilities geared to medium-size companies, in the form of specialized market segments and stock indices on the exchange. (In the long run, FIGs could attempt to realize values by concentrating on core businesses and selling off companies that are not related to the main business. In such a transformation, private placements with private equity funds/venture capital firms could play a role in streamlining the spin-off companies with an IPO as exit possibility.)

On the demand side, investors are influenced by perceptions of political and investment risk. Participation of domestic investors in the market is impeded by the absence of effective legal base for prevention of price manipulation and unfair market practices. The absence of the Law on Insider Trading, the lack of requirement of reporting under IFRS and the lack of independent verification and monitoring of effective adherence to the corporate governance code acts as a further deterrent to investor participation.

A significant share of trading in ADRs and GDRs originates from Russian corporations operating through offshore accounts. The rapid increase in the share of Russian equity turnover on foreign exchanges, primarily LSE, results from the inefficient infrastructure and high transactions costs on the domestic exchanges (See section II.2.7 below).

Negative trends:

— Market is highly concentrated 10 top stocks account for 76 percent of the total capitalization, liquidity is also concentrated in the blue chip stocks.
— Most gain in capitalization is due to price appreciation of blue chip stocks, particularly Gazprom.
— Mosenergo and Yukos gone from the list of blue chips.
— Liquidity is limited, above the average among emerging markets, but below Taiwan, Korea, Turkey, and Thailand.
— Free float is still low, between 5–25 percent.
— Shift in liquidity of Russian equities to London (up to 70 percent of turnover in 2004), through conversion of Russian equities into ADR, GDR and listing them in London, New York.
— Issuance of foreign SPV on Russian companies (e.g. Pyaterochka)—this equity cannot be traded in Russia.
— Over 90 percent of funds attracted through IPOs are international IPOs, domestic IPOs account for less than 10 percent (by value) in 2005.

Key Priorities Going Forward

Key policy reform priorities for the development of equity markets are as follows:

a. Adopt legislation on insider trading and price manipulation.
b. Improve regulation of hostile takeover.
c. Establish CD, introduce centralized settlement and clearing system.
d. Allow foreign securities trading though RDRs on MICEX and RTS.
e. Adopt calendar for IAS reporting for listed companies.
f. Enforce Governance Code criteria for listed companies.

Mutual Funds

Recent Evolution

Market Size and Structure

The investment funds industry has expanded significantly in the last five years, growing most dynamically in 2003–2005 period. Only starting from 2003, the investment funds began to play a noticeable role on the market. Overall, the number of registered and active unit investment funds (PIFs) grew from 28 by end 2000 to 396 by end 2005. The number of corporate investment funds (AIFs) has not changed by end 2005 (only in 2006 new corporate investment funds began to emerge). The NAV of both PIFs and AIFs grew from estimated Rub8.8 billion by end 2000 to estimated Rub235.8 billion by end 2005. The following table shows the growth of net asset value (NAV) for all types of investment funds and the growth in the number of unit investment funds (the most common form of funds) over the 2000–05 period.

The rapid growth of funds in the last three years was supported by favorable macroeconomic situation, increasing personal income, substantial improvements in the legal, regulatory, and supervision base for collective investments institutions, the ongoing pension reforms:

■ The macroeconomic factors included increasing ruble liquidity, increasing retained earnings and personal wealth, overall good performance of domestic equity and bond market.
■ Legal factors were the adoption of the Investment Fund Law (2001) and related secondary legislation regulating investment activities of the investment funds, related asset management companies, special depositaries (2002–05).

Figure 24. Investment Funds Growth

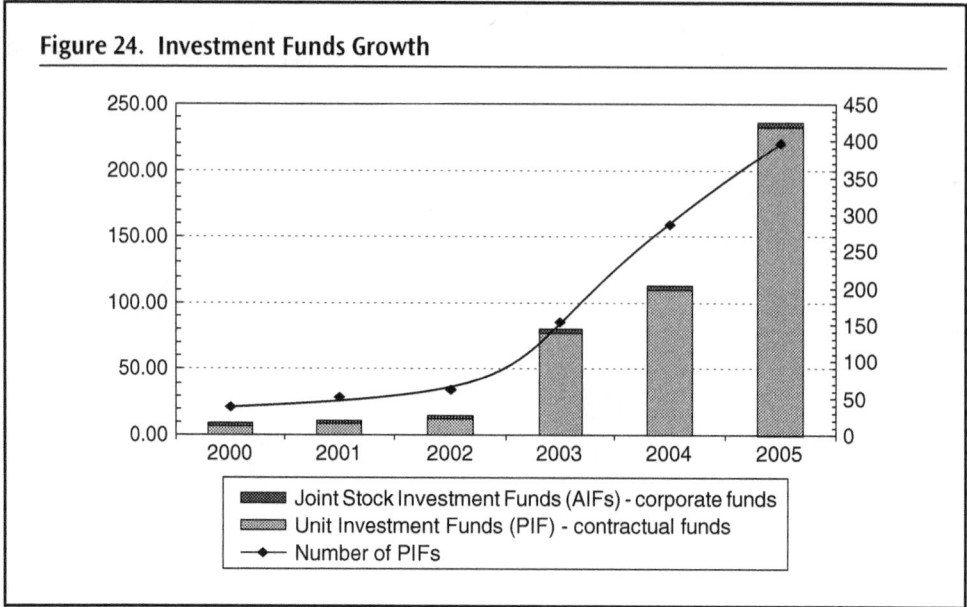

Source: National League of Asset Managers.

■ Taxation factors—improvements and clarification of the taxation of different types of investment funds.

A corporate investment fund is established in the form of a Russian opened joint stock company (OAO) and is called Joint-stock investment fund (AIF). The activity of AIF is subject to the general legislation applicable to join-stock companies. AIFs are prohibited from issuing securities other than ordinary shares sold through open subscription. AIF is managed by an asset management company (AMC).

A contractual investment fund or so-called Unit investment fund (PIF) is established in the form of pool of assets accumulated under the trust management agreement between the investor and the trust management company, AMC. PIF does not have a status of a legal entity and cannot fulfill any obligations related to the assets contained in the fund. The assets accumulated in PIFs are jointly owned by the investors. Purchase of a share (unit) of PIF by an investor is equivalent to a trust management between the investor and the fund's AMC. A PIF has can operate as "open-end" fund (shares are redeemed on a daily basis),"closed-end" fund (shares cannot be redeemed until the end of the term of the trust agreement) or "interval" fund (shares are redeemed at a term or interval set by the trust agreement).

The assets of all types of funds are held by a licensed "special depositary" (SD) for custody, safekeeping and control. Due to taxation regimes and other economic advantages, PIFs are a more popular structure than AIFs. The number of operating PIFs is growing rapidly while there are only three AIFs operating on the market—all transformed into AIFs from former (privatization) Voucher funds.[9] No new AIFs have been created since then.

PIFs are differentiated into three forms of funds by the possible timing of investment into open, interval and closed funds.

In terms of quantity, the number open-end funds grew most rapidly, followed by interval and closed-end funds. In terms of value, NAV, the closed-end funds grew most rapidly, followed by interval and open-end funds. The number of open-ended funds grew from about 19 in 2000 to 206 in 2005. The NAV of all open-ended funds increased from Rub0.36 billion by end 2000 to about Rub30.8 billion by end 2005. The number of interval funds grew from around 9 by end 2000 to 63 by end 2005, with their NAV expanding from Rub4.2 billion to Rub38.8 billion within the same period. Closed-end funds, legal based for which was built only in late 2002, begin to develop rapidly in 2003. The number of funds grew from three by end 2002 to 127 by end 2005. Their NAV increased most rapidly from Rub0.8 billion by end 2002 to Rub164.4 billion by end 2005.

Overall, the impressive growth in the size of mutual funds industry was largely attributed to the growth of closed-end funds, most of which were established by Russian corporations as an investment and tax saving vehicle. By end 2003, the NAV of closed-end funds accounted for 68 of the total PIFs value, compared to 21 percent for interval funds and 10 percent for open-end funds. By end 2005, the NAV of closed-end funds accounted for 70 percent of

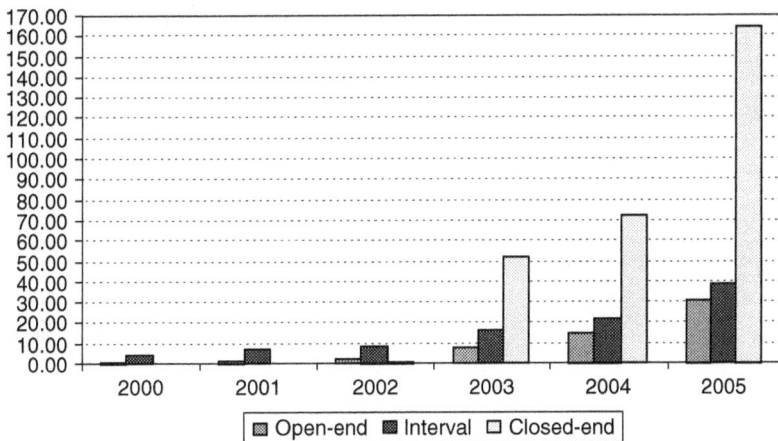

Figure 25. Investment Funds Net Asset Value (billions of rubles)

Source: Investfunds.ru.

---

9. At the end of 1998, all Voucher Funds were obliged to transform either into PIFs, AIFs or a joint stock company by January 1, 1999. As a result of reorganization, only five voucher funds chose to transform into PIFs and AIFs (two into PIFs and three into AIFs). Other voucher funds either seized their investment activities, or got their licenses revoked or joint other legal entities).

the value of all PIFs, compared to the 17 percent for interval funds, and the 13 percent for open-end funds.

In addition to the terms of investments, PIFs are also differentiated by the type of assets they can hold. Open, interval, and closed-end funds can be formed as equity funds (with minimum limit on equity investments), bond funds (with minimum limit on fixed income investments, mixed (or balanced) funds (with minimum limit on both equity and bond investments), index funds (investing primarily into equities, with the fund portfolio mimicking specific equity index), money market funds (investing primarily into money market securities). In addition to the above listed types of funds, closed-end funds can be formed as real estate funds (investing into real estate construction), venture funds (investing in venture projects), mortgage funds (investing in mortgage loans.) and direct investment funds (investing in projects). The latter four types of funds are essentially private equity funds.

Figure 26. Net Asset Value of Funds by Assets Types, End of 2005

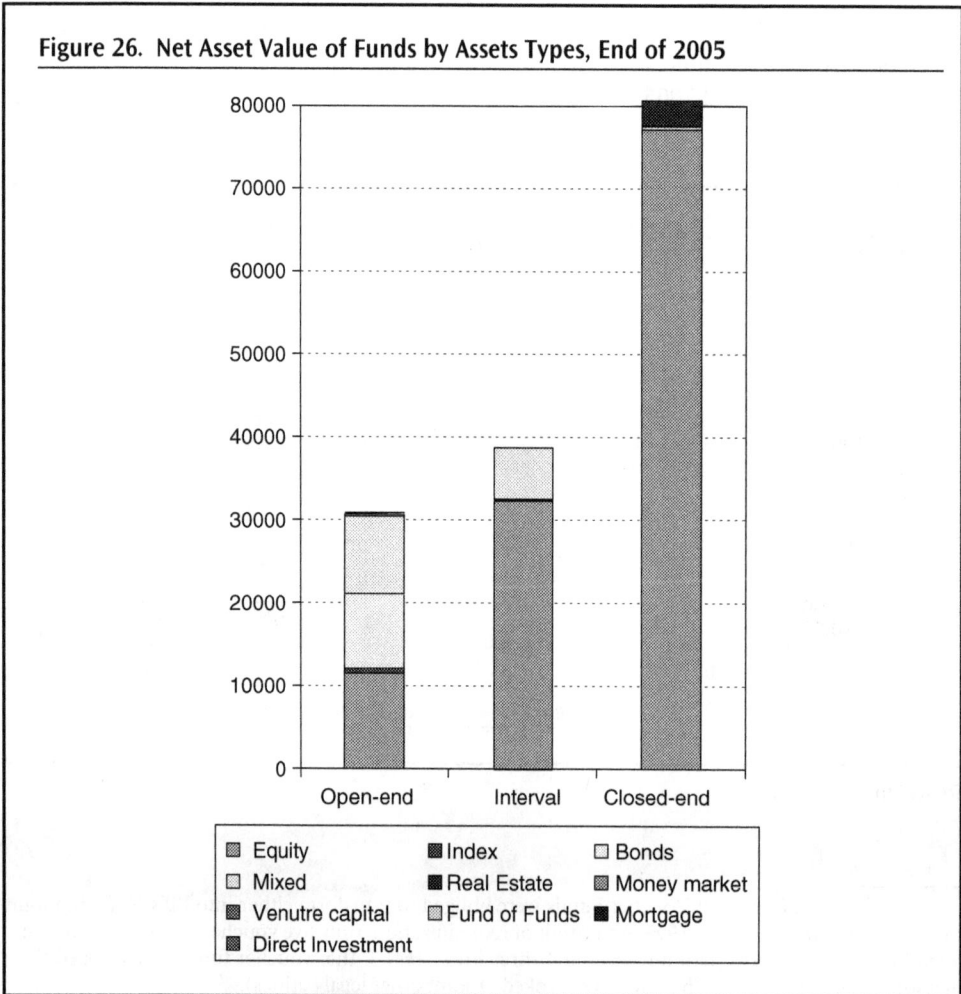

Source: National League of Asset Managers.

Figure 27. Number of Funds, End of 2005

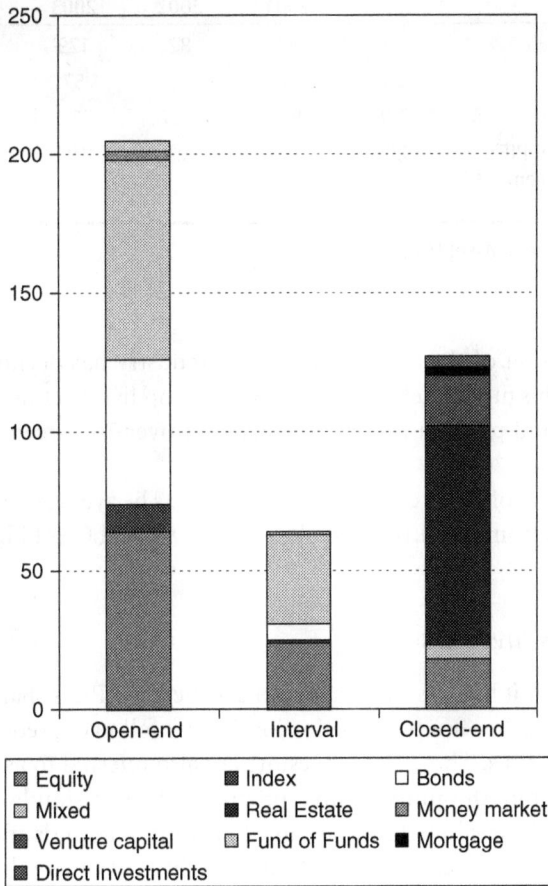

Legend:
- Equity
- Mixed
- Venutre capital
- Direct Investments
- Index
- Real Estate
- Fund of Funds
- Bonds
- Money market
- Mortgage

Source: National League of Asset Managers.

Most open and interval funds are formed as equity, bonds, or balanced. Most closed-end funds are formed, as equity, balanced, real estate, and bonds. Venture capital and index funds are also gaining popularity. Money market funds are rare. The new type of emerging funds are mortgage and direct investment funds. By the NAV of funds, equity funds dominate among open-end and interval funds, followed by balanced funds and bond funds. For closed-end funds, equity dominates as well, followed by real estate.

Both contractual and corporate investment funds are managed by professional asset management companies (AMC). The number of the licensed AMCs grew rapidly especially in the 2003–05 period, partially due to pension reform, as a result of which AMCs could obtain licensing to manage Pillar 2 pension funds (see pension section). About two-thirds of AMCs had mutual funds under management in 2004, while the other asset managers specialized on pension funds only.

Table 13: Concentration of Assets—Top Five Asset Management Companies

	2000	2001	2002	2003	2004	2005
Registered AMCs	28	42	82	129	178	237
AMCs with PIFs	23	28	31	57	103	134
PIFs NAV	7.0	9.1	12.7	77.1	109.9	230.9
Top 5 AMCs share of PIF's assets under management	95%	94%	92%	85%	71%	66.9%

Source: National League of Asset Managers.

The concentration of the asset management industry has declined in recent years, although still remains moderately concentrated. The top five asset managers that manage investment funds and pension funds accounted for over 70 percent of all assets under management in 2004.

The capitalization of funds continuous to increase. The average NAV of an investment funds has increased from Rub0.18 billion by end 2000 to Rub0.59 billion by end 2005.

Investment Funds Investors

Out of about 1300 unit holders of PIFs, over 1,200 become PIF's shareholders as a result of conversion of Voucher funds (privatization funds) following reorganization of some Voucher funds into PIFs. These 1200 investors are also referred to as "passive" investors since they did not buy the units in investment funds, but simply got their vouchers exchanged for units.[10] New investors that came to investment funds after 1999 are referred to as "market" investors since they voluntarily bought PIFs units. The number of "true" investors grew from around 6,000 by end of 2000 to nearly 122,000 by end September 2005 (see Table 14).

Table 14: Investment Funds Investors

	2000	2001	2002	2003	2004	Sep-05
PIFs Investors (excluding old investors of former voucher funds)	6,082	6,612	11,958	38,724	88,902	121,612

Source: Center for Capital Market Development.

---

10. Major investment funds based on Vaucher investors included (1) Alfa-capital PIF with about 1 million "passive" investors, (2) three Lukoil PIFs with about 100 thousand "passive" investors, (3) PIO Global AIF with about 100 thousand "passive" investors, and (4) "Zashita" and "Detstvo" AIFs with a few thousand "passive" investors.

Key Impediments to Development

The adoption of the Investment Funds Law ("the Law") in 2001 established a firm legal base for further development of the industry. The law clarified many of the established practices in the industry, such as mandatory disclosure rules on price, registration of prospectuses, licensing of managers, and minimum capital requirements set forth in the 1996 Presidential decree. The Law also included new provisions that allowed trading of funds on the secondary market and allowed the formation of closed-end funds. The Law also required the Federal Commission on Securities Market to establish operating procedures within the industry, including the definition of rights and obligations of asset management companies. Following the adoption of the Law, new amendments to the Securities Law (2002) and additional FSFM instructions further clarified some of operating procedures in the industry. The tax regime for PIFs was clarified by related instructions from the Ministry of Taxation and MOF. Following the abolishment of FCSM, the new regulator FSFM acquired regulatory and supervisory functions over investment funds. Because open-end and interval PIFs have no investor input into their management, they rely heavily on FSFM to assert their rights and protect their interests in the governance of the funds.

However, despite this progress, several deficiencies hamper the development of the investment fund industry going forward. Specifically:

(i) The FSFM only has authority to fine a joint-stock fund, Management Company, depository or other licensed entity under the Administrative Code. However, fines under the Administrative Code are insufficient. FSFM can also suspend the distribution of shares for a six-month period until the deficiencies, which FSFM has instructed the company to correct, have been eliminated. However, the Investment Funds Law does not give it the specific authority to annul the license of a registered, management company, investment trust, etc. This is true even though the Law appears to assume that the FSFM has such authority in various provisions in the Law.

(ii) More importantly, the Law does not contain any provisions, which would hold natural persons, who work for a legal entity, liable for violations of the Law acting individually or on behalf of the legal entity. This is a considerable gap in the Law since most violations are conducted by natural persons for their own gain.

(iii) In addition, FSFM is not given sufficient investigation authority to properly monitor the industry. While it can examine the books and records of a registrant fund, depositary, etc. FSFM cannot obtain documents from or question other individuals regarding the events in question ("third-parties") that are often critical to any securities investigation. However, FFMS does have an unusual authority to go into court on behalf of investors if the Law on Investment Funds has been violated by the management company, depository, agent or other licensed entities. The extent to which this provision in the Law is used, and the results that can be obtained for investors, is not yet fully developed.

(iv) The Law attempts to create an independent relationship between the external governance structures and a joint-stock investment fund by prohibiting a depository, registrar, auditor or appraiser of the assets of the joint-stock investment fund from also being shareholders in the fund. However, the Law does not prohibit a third entity, such as a financial conglomerate, from being a controlling shareholder in both entities. The same problem holds for the prohibitions against employees of the above entities from being on the board of directors of the joint-stock investment fund. However, the employees of a financial conglomerate, which holds stock in the fund, can hold such positions. These problems related to the lack of independence also apply to the relationship between a depository and a management company for investment trusts where the prohibitions are weaker and also allow for forms of common ownership.

Key Recommendations Going Forward

Based on the above, key policy priorities for the development of the investment fund industry are as follows:

(i) Strengthen enforcement powers of FSFM over investment funds and fund management companies, including authority to annul licenses and authority to apply fines.

(ii) Strengthen investigative powers of FSFM over funds, fund management companies and registrars.

(iii) Establish provisions holding natural persons liable for violations of the Law, acting individually or on behalf of a legal entity (fund, fund management company).

(iv) Strengthen independence between financial conglomerates and their employers and joint stock investment funds, unit investment funds, fund depositories, registrars and auditors.

Pension Funds

Recent Evolution

Pension Reform

In 2002, Russia began a far-reaching reform of its pension system, from a pay-as-you-go (PAYG), defined benefit (DB) mechanism to a three-pillar system, including a mandatory Pillar One covering basic pension, a mandatory Pillar Two including an insurance component and a funded (accumulative) component, and a voluntary, funded Pillar Three. However, significant problems remain concerning the future financial viability of the system and the provision of an adequate replacement rate.

The demands of the Russian pension system are substantial. The number of pensioners of the Pension Fund of Russia (PFR) increased steadily until 1998 when it stabilized at around 38 million individuals. As of the end of 2002, out of a population of 144 million, the number of contributors to the PAYG scheme amounted to 52 million, while the system provided pensions to about 39 million individuals, of which about half were old-age pensioners. Old-age pensions represented about 75–80 percent of the benefits paid for the period 1991–2002, with the remaining categories including invalidity, survivors, social pensions, military pensions and long service pensions.

The main characteristics of the pre-reform pension system in Russia are described in Box 1 later.

The new three-pillar system is described in Box 2. The system is the result of ongoing reforms and is still evolving. The key objectives of the reforms are:

■ Simplifying benefit formulas and removing generous eligibility criteria of the PAYG system;

Box 1: Pre-reform Pension System in Russia

Prior to the reform, the Russian pension system was dominated by a PAYG system administered by PFR. The system involved a complex eligibility and benefit structure. The system generally provided pensioners with a low level of income as evidenced by Table 1. Replacement rates were not only low, but also unstable due to arrears in the system and ad-hoc indexations of the benefits.

Table 15: Pension Replacement Rates and Other Indicators 1990–2000 (percent)

	1990	1991	1992	1993	1994	1995	1996	1997	1998	1999	2000
Pension replacement rate (old age pension to net wage)	33.7	33.8	25.8	33.6	35.0	39.8	38	39.5	36.4	28.3	30.8
Pension expenditure (as % of GDP)	6.0	6.6	7.3	6.4	5.9	5.5	5.8	6.9	6.0	5.6	
Average pension to MESI			1.2	1.4	1.3	1.0	1.2	1.1	1.1	0.7	
Minimum pension to MESI			0.85	0.78	0.66	0.48	0.73	0.76	0.67	0.40	

Note: The replacement rate is the pension income as a share of the previously earned wage net income.

Source: Kolosnitsyana & Topinska (2002); WB (2002).
MESI is Minimum Elderly Subsistence Income.

Despite low replacement rates, the large number of pensioners and small numbers of contributors created sustainability problems for the system. Before the introduction of the social tax, pension arrears in Russia represented 2 to 3 percent of GDP.

A major issue hampering a satisfactory performance of the Russian pension system prior to the reform was its low administrative capacity to manage pensions. In particular, the complex eligibility criteria and benefit formulas described above posed serious challenges to the PFR and its staff. The introduction of individual accounts was a major achievement but its concrete implementation proved difficult.

Prior to the reform, the PFR was responsible for the calculation and payments of pensions while the Central Tax Authority was in charge of contribution collection on the basis of a contribution rate of 29 percent (28 percent paid by employers and 1 percent paid by employees).

The legal status of the PFR in 2002 was inadequate, as it had not evolved according to the transfers of some of its responsibilities to the Central Tax Authorities. The accounting system, information flow and statistical base of the PFR also proved deficient thus, jeopardising the performance of the system as a whole.

The legislative framework governing the public pension system in Russia was very complex and was formed by over 50 different laws and legal acts. However, the far most important laws are:

Box 1: Pre-reform Pension system in Russia (*Continued*)

---

1. The Federal Law on State Pensions in the Russian Federation (20 November 1990),
2. The Federal Law on Pension Provision to Persons who conducted Military Service, Service in Internal Affairs, Offices and their Families (12 November 1993),
3. The Federal Law on Social Protection of Persons Victims of Radiation and Chernobyl Catastrophe (15 May 1992), and
4. The Federal Law on the Procedure for Calculating and Raising State Pensions (21 July 1997).

In 1992, private voluntary schemes were introduced in Russia offering annuities and programmed withdrawals, mainly within the framework of company plans. Some private pension funds also proposed schemes opened to individuals thus signing the development of a new culture in pension funding at the individual level.

- Increasing individual incentives to contribute to the system, thus ensuring fiscal solvency of the system by defining clear distribution/insurance/savings objectives in the benefit formula; and
- Increasing the level of pension benefits by diversifying pension arrangements and deepening financial and capital markets.

The new benefit formula reflects the shift from a DB scheme to a defined contribution (DC) system, which partially mitigates the sustainability problems. The new three-pillar system is composed of the following components:

- A basic part (Pillar I), consisting of a fixed amount approved by the Government and financed by the mandatory PAYG scheme (Rub953 since August 2005) (Pillar I, un-funded);
- A mandatory insurance part (Pillar II), consisting of an annuity calculated on the basis of the pension capital divided by the expected pension period (NDC benefit) (Pillar II, unfunded);
- An accumulative part, that is, pension savings divided by the expected pension period (Pillar II, funded); and
- Ultimately, it will be possible to derive additional pension revenues from Pillar III for those who pay voluntary contributions to a Non-State Pension Fund.

As seen above, despite the reform, the eligibility criteria of the PAYG system do not provide adequate incentives to workers to contribute to the system. The replacement rate of the basic benefit is expected to decline rapidly to reach 8–10 percent in the next decade; retirement age is not increased and therefore does not ensure an adequate contribution period; the notional rate of return of the NDC scheme remains very low, and the replacement rate of the NDC scheme is also declining with time.

Pension payments for the first and second Pillar are paid from the Budget of the Pension Fund of Russia (PFR), which is financed by the pension component of the United Social Tax (UST) and Reserves of the PFR. The United Social Tax (US$) is the main source of the PFR funds. Pillar I and II pension is financed by the pension component of the UST.

Box 2: Overview of the Russian Pension System, Starting from January 1, 2005		
Pillar I	**Pillar II**	**Pillar III**
MANDATOR BASIC PART	MANDATORY INSURANCE PART	VOLUNTARY PART
Based on PAYG principle.	Based on PAYG principle.	(Non-state voluntary pension)
Financed by the Federal Budget (including Unified Social Tax paid by employers). State governed.	Financed by portion of Unified Social Tax paid by employers. State governed.	Based on funded principle.
Paid only to retired individuals with at least 5 years of work record.	Subject to adjustments as per inflation rates and increase of average wage.	Financed by voluntary contributions to a NSPF.
Subject to adjustments as per inflation rates.	FUNDED or ACCUMULATIVE PART	Invested by the NSPF.
Tends to reach the "subsistence wage."	Based on funded principle:	Pension amount depends on the voluntary contributions paid.
Minimum requirements for the size of the basic part (Rub953 since August 2005).	Calculated for individuals born after 1967. Accumulated pat to be invested either by the State Asset Manager, or by a private Asset Manager, or by a Non-State Pension Fund of the insured's choice.	
	Only due to the eligible individuals born after 1966.	

Source: ING Pension website available at: http://www.ingnpf.ru.

Following recent amendments to the Law "On Obligatory Pension Insurance" and the Tax Code of the Russian Federation (Article 24.2), the maximum UST rate is decreased from 35.6 to 26 percent of the payroll as of January 1, 2005. As a result of these change the pension component of the UST is be reduced from 28 percent (of 35.6 percent UST) to 20 percent (of 26 percent UST).

As of end 2005, UST tax rate is 26 percent, broken down into 20 percent pension component, and 6.6 percent other needs; 6 percent of the pension component goes for Pillar 1 and 14 percent for Pillar 2. People born prior to 1967 do not have a funded component of Pillar 2—all funds assigned to Pillar 2 for these individuals go to insurance part of pension. People born after 1966, have both insurance and funded component of the Pillar 2. (As of end 2005, 14 percent assigned for Pillar 2 split at 10 percent insurance part and 4 percent funded part; Starting from 2008, only 8 percent would go to the insurance part and 6 percent would go to the funded part.)

The generous eligibility criteria inherited from the previous system are being reformed. Retirement age remains at 60 for men and 55 for women.[11] Early retirement pensions are maintained in the new system with 15 categories of workers entitled to early retirement pensions. Early retirement pensions are also granted to 13 categories of individuals justifying

---

11. Currently draft law is prepared to increase the retirement age to 63 for men and 60 for women.

Table 16: The Reform of the Unified Social Tax (US$) and Its Influence on the Pension Reform

Rates as of January 1, 2005	Annual income	<280,000 RUB		280,000–600,000 RUB	>600,000 RUB
	Applicable UST rate	26%		10%	2%
Rates prior to January 1, 2005	Annual income	<100,000 Rub	100,000–300,000 RUB	300,000–600,000 RUB	>600,000 RUB
	Applicable UST rate	35.6%	20%	10%	2%

Source: ING Pension Newsletter No 19—September 2004.

adequate length of service such as mothers of five children or more, teachers, workers in the North, and so forth. In addition, minimum contribution periods have been reduced from 20–25 years of contribution years to only five years. Young retirement age, early retirement pensions, and shorter contribution periods put pressure on the financial viability of the system.

In 2003–04 the full benefits of multi-pillar system became available for working male born in 1953 or later and female born in 1957 or later. Following the recent amendments to the Law on "Obligatory Pension Insurance," the middle age category of working population (men born between 1953 and 1966, women born between 1957 and 1966) will be excluded from the eligible group as of January 1, 2005. Only individual born after 1966 will be eligible for the funded component of Pillar 2.

The funded part of pillar II is accumulated under this new pension scheme in the Pension Fund of Russia (PFR), which is responsible for:

a. Collecting pension contributions;
b. Posting pension contributions to individual accounts;
c. Transferring pension contributions to eligible asset managers and NSPF in accordance with appropriate government regulations; and
d. Posting appropriate investment income to individual accounts.

In 2002, the new pension system was introduced at the level of Russian corporations that were required to calculate the Unified Social Tax payments in a new way to include the accumulative component of individual pension savings. At the same time, PFR started to collect pension contributions and post them to individual accounts. The funded pillar II accumulated in the PFR began to be managed by the State Asset Management Company (Vnesheconombank).

In 2003, the pension reform was introduced at the level Russian citizens, as they were granted the right to select from 55 qualified private asset management company (AMC) to manage the funded potion of Pillar 2, which officially still remained the property of the State.

The Notification Letter was sent to eligible citizens, including a the statement of their individual account balance with PFR and a special form that allowed eligible individuals to select an asset manager to manage the accumulative portion of their pension. Delays in the distribution of the Notification Letter and lack of public information on the reform led to the failure of the pension reform awareness campaign in 2003. The majority of Russian citizens either failed to understand the essence of the pension reform or were unaware of them. As a result, only 2 percent of eligible citizens decided to transfer the funds to the private sector, while 98 percent did not return the Notification Letter and, as a result, their accumulations stayed with the State AMC (Vnesheconombank).

In principle, only appropriately regulated asset managers should have been eligible to manage resources of the funded Pillar II scheme in 2003. The actual selection of 55 asset managers, however, has been much criticized as non-transparent and biased. The selection criteria for asset managers under the funded scheme was the following:

- Asset managers are selected by tender;
- Asset managers must be Russian legal entities, but can have Russian or foreign ownership; and
- Asset managers must have a signed agreement with a Specialized Depository (custodian) authorized by the PFR.

From 2004, NSPFs are also allowed to qualify for managing funds of pillar II. The requirements for NSPFs willing to participate in pillar II are more exacting than for asset managers but their role is growing rapidly as they represent a good compromise between a conservative state asset manager and private asset managers. In 2004, 77 non-state pension funds were allowed to participate in the management of the accumulative part of Pillar II. Eligible citizens were allowed to choose among both 55 AMCs and 77 non-state pension funds. In case of the NSPF, the transfer of funds included also the transfer of the ownership from the state to the NSPF. However, due to various bureaucratic delays and recent cut in the eligible group, transfer of fund to private sector was not significant in 2004 either. To date only captive NSPF and their related asset management companies were able to attract significant number of accounts using their administrative capacity over existing corporate pension programs. However, most of these companies failed to attract retail clientele. Moreover, many non-captive firms find it economically ineffective to participate in Pillar 2 schemes under current legal requirements on the investment of the Pillar 2 funds.

Overall, the pension reforms intended to gradually move funded Pillar 2 component from the public sector (PFR) to private sector (AMCs and NSPFs) where they could be managed more effectively. So far transfer of funds to private sector was unsuccessful, partially due to poor pension reform awareness campaign, tax distortions and various bureaucratic delays that prevented AMCs and NSPFs to successfully compete with VEB. Out of Rub239.9 billion accumulated by PFR by end of 2005, only about 2.5 percent was managed by private sector (AMCs and NSPFs; see Table 17). The rest of funds are managed by the VEB on behalf of the PFR that can only invest into government securities.

The funded portion of Pillar 2 funds can be invested into state bonds with no limits, sub-sovereign bonds (up to 40 percent), corporate bonds and stocks (with increasing limits in 2005–07; see Table 18).

Pillar II also includes the possibility of occupational pension plans. The basic principle of these schemes is that employers make an additional contribution to a NSPF of their

Table 17: Funded Part of Pillar II (billions of rubles)

Year	Pillar II, Funded	Funds Managed by State (PFR and State AMC)	Funds Managed by Private Sector (Private AMC and NSPF)
2002	33.7	33.7	0.0
2003	81.5	81.5	0.0
2004	158.9	155.7	3.2
2005	239.9	234.0	5.9

Source: PFR, FSFM data, WB Staff calculations.

choice or directly to the PFR with two levels of contributions: 5 percent for hard work and 12 percent for very hard work, these levels being determined by a special commission. However, the legislative framework of the new pension system regarding mandatory occupational pension systems, insurance premiums for funding the above systems, and on financing of the funded part of labor pension benefits has not yet been completed.

Uncertain Replacement Rates in the Long Run. Since January 1, 2002, the PFR recalculated all types of pension benefits according to the parameters of the reformed system. As a result, pension benefits and labor pensions have been increased significantly in real terms. Despite these developments, replacement rates produced by the system will not be sustainable in the long run. According to World Bank estimates (2002), replacement rates are projected to fall from 36 percent in 2002 to 19 percent in 2050. The main factor contributing to this decline is the indexation method used for both the basic and NDC schemes.

System surpluses, which are projected to amount to 1.1 percent of GDP in 2050, could be used to increase replacement rates. However, projections show that, if the system balance were to be safeguarded, the use of surpluses could only increase replacement rates to 28–29 percent in the next 10–15 years, followed by a decline to 21 percent in subsequent years. Conversely, if replacement rates under the reformed system were to be maintained around 30 percent, projections indicate that this would create a fiscal deficit amounting to 2 percent of the GDP after 2015.

Table 18: Investment Rules for Funded Portion of Pillar 2, Managed by Private Sector

	2004	2005	2006	2007
State bonds		No limit		
Regional bonds		Up to 40%		
Municipal bonds		Up to 40%		
Corporate bonds	Up to 50%	Up to 60%	Up to 70%	Up to 80%
Stock	Up to 40%	Up to 45%	Up to 55%	Up to 65%

Source: FSFM.

Precarious Fiscal Sustainability. According to World Bank estimates (2002), the pension system is fiscally sustainable except in a pessimistic scenario.[12] However, this result is subject to important caveats:

- The overall fiscal sustainability of the reform is strongly correlated with economic and productivity growth: in the pessimistic scenario envisaging an economic slow-down, the PAYG system is subject to significant deficits, requiring important fiscal transfers to keep it in balance;
- The fiscal sustainability of the pension system requires that the surpluses of the basic benefit scheme be used to finance the projected deficits of the Notional Defined Contribution (NDC; the new pillar II) scheme. These deficits are created by a generous initial notional capital provided to all workers who switch to the NDC and by the decline in the Russian population; and
- The fiscal solvency of the pension system under the base and optimistic scenarios is achieved only through a decline in pension replacement rates, thus posing a significant political problem for the Government in the long run.

Administrative Difficulties. The reform creates a significant administrative challenge. Preparatory work was done in 2002 to formulate the required legislative and regulatory framework, to set up respective databases at the federal level with use of modern information technologies covering the insurers and the insured (including pensioners) and to implement computerized technologies to perform the basic procedures defined by the new pension legislation. Achievements so far include:

- Transfer of the functions of pension benefit assessment and payment to the territorial bodies of the PFR and creation of a unified centralized administration system to manage the mandatory pension insurance funds.[13]
- Creation of an individual accounts database systematically recording updated data of over 110 million insured individuals (employed workers, including self-employed, unemployed, students over 14 years old, non-working pensioners) with information about their pension rights.
- Development of a client servicing in pension provision bodies including: client services, consultation stations at enterprises, mobile consultation stations.
- Improvement of the information provided to the PFR beneficiaries: in 2003, over 41 million of individual account statements covering the state of the special (funded) part of the individual accounts were prepared and delivered. A mechanism of reconciliation of individual accounts and accounting data was developed and implemented in 2002 to ensure that data provided to beneficiaries are correct. Besides individual account statements the mailed package included a form of application for statement of a choice of an investment portfolio (asset management company).

---

12. Pension Reform in Russia: Design and Implementation, 2002. Although the results are viewed as broadly valid, they should be interpreted with caution, since conditions may have changed since the study was conducted. Three scenarios were assessed: base case, optimistic and pessimistic scenarios.

13. RF Presidential Decree No. 1709 of September 27, 2000 on Measures Aimed at Improvement of State Pension Provision Administration in the Russian Federation.

About 500,000 insured persons received statements of zero balance on the special part of their individual accounts. This allows the insured person who received such notification to apply to the employer-insurer for clarification of the reasons of nonpayment of the insurance premiums.

Despite this progress, several administrative challenges remain:

(a) Tracking each worker's lifetime contributions to the system to ensure a timely and exact retribution on accumulated contributions throughout the working life of contributors.
(b) Ensuring greater accountability of the agencies managing the funded component of the system as their financial actions will directly influence pensions' replacement rates.
(c) Developing an effective and continuous collaboration between the agency in charge of contribution collection and the agency in charge of data management. This is particularly important in the reformed pension system, as workers cannot be credited for deposits to their personal funded account unless their contributions are actually transferred to the pension fund.[14]

Non-State Pension Funds and Retirement Benefit Schemes (Pillar III)

Since their introduction in 1992, the number of non-state pension funds (NSPFs) grew to 290 by the end of 2000 and declined slightly to 260 by end of 2005, as some of the fund's licenses were cancelled or revoked due to the non-compliance with NSPFs' requirements. On the qualitative site, the pension reserves (pillar 3 funds) of the non-state pension funds (NSPFs) grew rapidly in the last five years, increasing from Rub15.6 billion by end 2000 (about 0.2 percent of GDP) to nearly Rub200 billion by the end of the third quarter 2005 (estimated 1 percent of GDP). The average pension reserves of funds has increased substantially from less than US$2 million by end 2000 to about US$27 million by end September 2005. At the same time, the sector remains heterogeneous and concentrated, with 10 NSPFs' reserves exceeding US$80 million and about half of funds with reserves lower than US$1 million. The largest NSPFs have been established and maintained by the largest Russian enterprises. The assets allocation of the pension reserves of the major NSPF—to invest into stocks and bonds, especially parent company stock, bank deposits of affiliated banks.

By end September 2005, NSPFs covered 5.9 million people or roughly 8 percent of the economically active population. Most of these, however, are covered indirectly through corporations, which account for more than 90 percent of the client base and about 99 percent of contributions.

As of the end 2003, only slightly more than 600,000 people came to pension funds independently. One of the reasons for this low figure is the high cost of private pension funds, which are highly taxed, thus making non-state pension schemes only attractive for companies. At this stage, the ability of NSPFs to substantially raise pension replacement

---

14. Pension Reform in Russia: Design and Implementation, 2002.

Table 19: NSPF Sector (Pillar III Funds)

	2000	2001	2002	2003	2004	9m 2005
Number of private pension funds	291	257	284	285	270	263
NSPFs Own assets, Rub billion						
Pension Reserves, Rub billion	15.6	33.6	51.4	89.6	169.8	198.9
as % of GDP	0.2%	0.4%	0.5%	0.7%	1.0%	1.0%
Participants, million	3.3	4.0	4.4	5.3	5.5	5.9
Participants receiving payments, million	0.3	0.3	0.4	0.4	0.5	0.7
Private pension payments, Rub billion	0.6	1.0	2.0	3.3	5.0	5.3

Source: Federal Financial Market Service.

rates remains low with an average benefit of 656 rubles at the end of 2003 (or 37 percent of the average size of labor pension).

The welfare increasing potential of private pensions also depends on the structure of NSPFs portfolios. Available data at this point suggest that NSPF portfolios are heavily dominated by equities. This raises concerns over the financial security and the rate of return on assets accumulated by NSPFs. In addition, this indirectly confirms that the role of NSPF has been so far mainly to provide financing for large enterprises capital and investment project, rather than providing an optimal, prudent combination of assets where individual pension savings could be invested to further protect them in old age. At present, more than 30 percent of NSPFs contributions are usually re-invested in the founding company. There is a feeling that NSPFs have abused their non-profit status, and that they should become commercial, for profit, transparent organizations, more visible to possible investors, and to bring their tax status in line with the world recognized EET (Exempt, Exempt, Taxable)[15] principle of taxation of pensions. This would allow pension funds to be sold and bought more easily, and lead to a consolidation of the industry.

Key Impediments to the Future Development of NSPFs

The legal and regulatory framework for transition from mandatory pay-as-you-go pension to Pillar One (basic part of mandatory pension) and Pillar Two (insurance and funded parts) has been mostly completed by end 2004. The eligibility criteria for private AMCs, NSPFs, state AMCs, and special depositaries have been established and rules of accumulation of the funded portion of Pillar Two have been defined. The next step of pension reform is to clear all the outstanding issues related to the investment rules of the funded portion of the Pillar 2 (concentration of assets in PFR, low activity of eligible individual in selection

---

15. This is the tax regime that exempts contributions from tax, and fund income, but does tax the pension in payment.

of AMC for management of their pension accumulations, lack of investment instruments, taxation issues, limits on investments into the founding company, and so forth).

Weakness of Regulatory Framework

NSPFs are insufficiently regulated and supervised, and have an non-transparent legal nature and policies. Thus, the trust of savers in these mechanisms could be easily lost and is still not very high, whereas, on the other hand they tend to be company plans, run and fuelled by large employers, and they tend to be used as a source of financing of company shares and investment, rather as a mechanism to optimise returns for beneficiaries while minimizing risk. Market-based pension funds are very limited in number.

The establishment of FFMS and its acquisition of the regulatory and supervisory activities of the former NSPF Inspection Department (ID) at the Ministry of Labour and Social Development provides an opportunity to strengthen the regulatory and supervisory framework for NSPFs, and to gain the public's trust in these institutions.

Protection of Contributors' Rights

One of the determinants of NSPF development is the degree of trust from the general public in the products offered, the mechanisms, management and investment of accumulated assets. In particular, the issue of contributors' rights is crucial to create trust in NSPF.

The Basic Principles of private occupational pension schemes regulation,[16] formulated by the International Network of Pension Regulators and Supervisors (INPRS) stipulate that (Principle N   3):

■ Private pension funds shall have free access never discriminated on the grounds of age, payroll, gender, seniority, conditions of employment, part-time employment, and social status.
■ Regulation shall ensure that vested rights are protected and rights to pension fixed, no matter who contributes to the scheme, employee or employer. There must be positive encouragement to index pension funds and pensions.
■ Rights to pension shall be "portable" (rights to pension shall survive any change of employment) to maintain professional mobility. Members of a pension scheme must be protected through various mechanisms in case of early retirement.

Much remains to be done in this respect in Russia as both the legal framework and regulatory mechanisms do not adequately ensure the respect of these measures. Several rights such as vested rights are only regulated on an ad-hoc and case-by-case basis, leaving them to arbitrary management.

Public Awareness and Information Disclosure

Finally, a challenge that needs to be faced in order to ensure the smooth development of the NSPF sector in Russia pertains to: (i) increasing awareness of the Russian general public

---

16. Source: www.pensionreform.ru, www.inprs.org.

on NSPFs activities and products, and (ii) ensuring a transparent information disclosure to all participants of private retirement benefit schemes.

Despite the increase in the number of clients in the NSPF sector, most Russian people are not aware at all of NSPF activities and private retirement benefit schemes, and the few who do know about them are usually fairly suspicious. In this respect, increasing NSPFs information disclosure is crucial. At present, NSPF are required to provide a large volume of information to the NSPF Inspection as part of their reporting duties. However, this information is not disclosed to the public at large, thus creating an information gap that is only filled by mistrust in NSPF.

Key Priorities Going Forward

Key policy reform priorities for the development of the private pension industry are as follows:

- Strengthen the capacity of the pension administration to track each worker's lifetime contribution to the system to ensure timely and exact retribution on accumulated contributions throughout the working life of contributors.
- Ensure greater accountability of the agencies managing the funded component of the system as their financial actions will directly affect pensions' replacement rates.
- Strengthen collaboration between the agency in charge of contributions collection and the agency in charge of data management.
- Broaden the list of financial instruments eligible for the investments of PFR.
- Strengthen regulation and supervision of NSPFs in accordance wit international standards.
- Establish and enforce comprehensive disclosure rules for NSPFs.
- Strictly limit the share of NSPF portfolio that can be invested in the NSPF founding company.
- Broaden the list of financial instruments eligible for the investments of PFR.

Insurance Companies

Recent Evolution

The role of insurance companies as institutional investors on capital markets increased significantly in 2004–05. These were attributed mainly to three factors. First, enacted in early 2004 amendments to the Federal Insurance Law set the new requirements for the minimum paid-in authorised capital of insurance companies and established procedure for specialization of companies on life or non-life insurance. Second, the share of tax optimisation schemes, especially in life insurance has contracted significantly in the last two years due to changes in the law and improved enforcement of the law by insurance regulator. Third the introduction of the mandatory third party liability auto insurance has helped insurance companies increase true premiums collected in 2004–05.

Market Size and Structure

The Russian insurance sector has grown steadily over the past five years. According to official statistics, gross insurance premiums have grown from Rub171 billion in 2000 to Rub472 billion in 2004.[17] In relation to GDP, market penetration has grown from 0.7 percent in 1993 to around 2.8 percent in 2004. According to Federal Statistics Service, around 250–300 thousand people are occupied in the insurance sector.

    The structure of the market has evolved considerably over the last few years. According to official statistics, in 2000, 82 percent of the market consisted of voluntary insurance, of which over half was life insurance, about a third property insurance, followed by other

---

17. Official statistics on 2005 insurance sector performance is not available as of March 2006.

than personal and the liability insurance. Between 2000 and 2004, the share of voluntary insurance declined from 82 to 76 percent, of which life insurance accounted for 45 percent and property insurance 38 percent. Within the same time period the share of compulsory insurance increased from 18 to 24 percent of the total, of which medical insurance accounted for 72 percent, followed by motor third party liability at 24 percent. With the adoption of the law on compulsory motor third party liability in July 2003, the share of compulsory insurance is expected to increase substantially.

A significant share of the voluntary life and property insurance is constituted of tax avoidance schemes such as wage schemes. Under life insurance schemes, employers provide compensation for their workers and avoid the burden of social and other taxes on that compensation. Insurance contracts are surrendered within a short period following payment of the premium. This translates into aberrant claims to premium ratios that are ranging between 89.0 percent in 1999 and 131.0 percent in 2002. Based on an analysis of the performance of the top 100 insurance companies, the EU TACIS 2002 insurance market survey estimated that the size of the life insurance market outside wage schemes is about US$500 million in 2001 (Rub15.7 billion), or about 11 percent of total life insurance including wage schemes. Under property insurance schemes, companies use property insurance payments as additional losses to reduce tax claims. The introduction of new tax rules in 2003, together with an industry campaign promoted by ARIA (All Russian Insurance Association), with the support of the EU TACIS Program, have reportedly reduced the impact of wage schemes, and most of the biggest companies are now gradually abandoning this "gray" market, having understood the importance of transparency and good reputation for the healthy growth of the sector. While several small companies are still providing these services, an effective implementation of the recently introduced minimum capital requirements should force them out of the market.

The insurance market at about 2.8 percent of GDP in 2004 appears to be about average among the study countries. It is about half the market penetration in the CE3 countries, and is significantly below the ECA Region average. By contrast, it is less than a fourth of the market penetration in the EU-15 countries and in the OECD countries, about a fifth of the market penetration of the US and Japan and a tenth that of the United Kingdom.

Insurance Companies: Profile and Performance

The number of insurance companies grew rapidly from about 1500 companies in 1993 to about 2300 companies in 1997. Following the 1998 crisis, massive bankruptcies led to a precipitous fall in the number of companies to their 1993 level by the end of 1999. In the following years, the number of companies has stabilized at around 1400. The industry is highly fragmented, with the top three insurers controlling less than 25 percent of the sector vs. an average of 50 to 70 percent in East European countries. The presence of a large number of small insurance companies with low levels of capital points to weak regulation and overly liberal solvency requirements, reducing the incentives for consolidation and opening opportunities for companies involved in tax avoidance schemes. Domestic insurance companies dominate the sector.

Overall sector profitability as measured by the crude loss ratio (CLR) fluctuates between 63.7 percent in 1999 and 65 percent in 2003. Profitability varies greatly among

Table 20: Insurance Sector Profitability—Crude Loss Ratio, Percent

	1999	2000	2001	2002	2003
Voluntary	0.574	0.654	0.57	0.724	0.632
Personal	0.81	0.87	0.74	1.15	0.95
Life	*0.89*	*0.93*	*0.8*	*1.31*	*1.05*
Personal non-life	0.5	0.538	0.46	0.617	0.6
Property	0.249	0.215	0.148	0.163	0.187
Liability	0.112	0.091	0.098	0.148	0.186
Compulsory	0.86	0.914	0.923	0.953	0.742
Non-Life (Voluntary + Compulsory)	*0.74*	*0.5*	*0.44*	*0.49*	*0.45*
Total	0.637	0.701	0.621	0.771	0.658

Source: Federal Service for State Statistics.

insurance products. At one end of the spectrum, aberrant CLRs above 100 percent in 2002–2003 are observed in the life insurance sector, reflecting the high incidence of tax avoidance schemes. At the other end, CLRs remain below 20 percent in liability insurance. Several insurance products show an improving profitability situation in recent years. This is the case of non-life products in general (voluntary and compulsory), with CLR declining from 74 percent in 1999 to 45 percent in 2003. Within non-life, property insurance shows a marked improvement with CLR dropping from 25 percent in 1999 to 19 percent in 2003 (see Table 20).

The investment portfolio of insurance companies has shown a rapid diversification away from government bonds toward higher risk-higher yield investments, in particular corporate and sub-sovereign bonds. As of mid 2005, insurance companies investment into corporate and sub-sovereign bonds is estimated at about 19 percent of the total demand (Troika Dialog estimate).

Reinsurance has been growing steadily in 2000–03. The geographical destination of reinsurance is heavily skewed toward the Baltic countries, which account for about two thirds of the total. The dominance of the Baltics as destination for reinsurance as opposed to major established OECD reinsurance markets may be an indicator of the incidence of money laundering in the sector.

Key Impediments to the Development of the Insurance Sector

Separation Between Life and Non-life Insurance

The New Law On Insurance (adopted in late 2003, enforced in early 2004) amends the 1993 Law on Insurance ("the Law") (Article 3) restates the basic distinction between voluntary and compulsory insurance, in keeping with article 927 of the Russian Civil Code, and specifies that Federal laws establishing new types of compulsory insurance must clearly spell out certain basic elements of the contract.[18] The effective separation between life and non-life operations will be achieved only in 2007, while starting from the time in which these new amendments entered into force insurance companies are under a duty to stop writing either of the two businesses and to notify the supervisory body of their choice. Accordingly, a comprehensive re-licensing of existing companies is set to take place in 2007.

Capital Requirements

The New Insurance Law introduces higher capital requirements for insurance companies operating in the Russian market. In case of non-compliance, licenses will be revoked. As mentioned above, according to the data provided by the supervisory authority, as of January 1, 2004, 1397 licensed insurance companies in the Russian market, most of which are considered to be undercapitalized and poorly managed. An effective enforcement of the newly established capital requirements, therefore, is likely to result in a substantial reduction of the number of insurance companies. The Federal Insurance Supervision Service (FISS) estimates that only 400–500 companies will be able to fulfill the new requirements, but representatives of All-Russian Insurance Association (AIRA) are concerned that several small insurance companies will provide false bank statements as a proof of their compliance. The supervisory authority, therefore, will face quite a difficult task in making accurate crosschecks.

Actuarial Assessment of Reserves

Under the New Insurance Law, insurance companies are required to carry out an actuarial assessment of their reserves and to file an actuarial report together with their annual financial statements starting from July 1, 2007. This provision has the potential to bring about a significant improvement in the current reserving, risk assessment and risk management practices. Nevertheless, the availability of a sufficient number of qualified actuaries is currently uncertain and this will constitute a major challenge for the Russian insurance market in the coming years.

Compulsory Motor Third Party Liability Insurance (MTPL)

Compulsory motor third party liability (MTPL) insurance was introduced by Federal Law n.40-FZ of April 25, 2002 on Compulsory Insurance against the Civil Liability of Owners of Transport Vehicles (with amendments of December 24, 2002 and June 23, 2003), in force since July 2003. While the compulsory nature of MTPL will certainly expand the market for this class of insurance and the total amount of gross premiums written in the

---

18. The list of elements in article 3, item 4, includes: (a) insurance businesses; (b) the objects subject to insurance; (c) a list of insurable events; (d) the minimal insured amount or the procedure for assessing it; (e) the rate, structure or procedure for setting the insurance tariff; (f) the term and procedure for the payment of insurance premium (insurance contribution); (g) the effective term of a contract of insurance; (h) the procedure for assessing the amount of insurance compensation; (i) the monitoring of insurance practices; (j) the consequences of a default on or improper performance of obligations by insurance businesses; (k) other provisions.

non-life segment, several operating problems must be fully taken into account. First, insurance companies must recognize that MTPL will soon give rise to a very high number of claims, requiring substantial investments and expenses in order to ensure sound and proper claims handling practices; the number of claims might also constitute a serious problem for the Russian court system. Second, claims reserves must be properly kept and accounted for (especially IBNR reserves), in light of the long-tail nature of liabilities in this field. Third, there is a compelling need to set up a proper system to combat fraud in the automobile sector: to this purpose, ARIA reported that there is a plan to develop a database of information aimed at monitoring and preventing fraudulent conducts. The current practice to require the intervention of a police officer in case of any car accident, even if no personal injury is involved, already proved to be highly ineffective and unbearable: for minor accident "amicable settlement forms" should be introduced instead. It is not clear whether domestic insurance companies have gained full and proper understanding of these problems and, therefore, future developments of the MTPL market should be closely monitored by the supervisory authority.

Foreign Participation

A progressive easement of the severe limitations to foreign participation in the Russian insurance market initially set forth in the early nineties was brought about as a result of bilateral agreements with the european community and wto accession negotiations. Pursuant to the Law on Insurance of 1993, the participation of foreign capital in Russian insurance companies was limited to 49 percent. This rule has been subsequently waived by amendments introduced in 1999, in compliance with the Partnership and Co-operation Agreement (PCA) signed with the European Community on June 24, 1994. At the same time, however, new limitations affecting foreign-owned companies were introduced, including substantially higher capital requirements, an overall limit of 15 percent of total foreign capital in the Russian insurance market, the prohibition to write life insurance and compulsory insurance classes, and the requirement to have Russian citizens as CEO and chief accountant.

Starting from 2004, the maximum total quota of foreign capital allowed in the Russian market has been raised to 25 percent, even if it should be pointed out that, at present, foreign participation amounts to less than 3 percent of total aggregate authorized capital, according to the most recent data provided by the supervisory authority.[19] More importantly, under the law, all limitations have been waived for insurance companies participated (or fully owned) by foreign investors belonging to member states of the European Community. All other foreign insurers and investors, however, are still subject to the aforementioned limitations. In addition, cross border direct insurance, as well as and branching, are still prohibited in Russia.

Consumer Protection

From a legislative and regulatory point of view, the lack of public confidence and trust in the insurance sector may be addressed by way of increased transparency requirements—

---

19. The data provided by the Federal Insurance Supervision Service (FISS) indicate that the share of foreign capital in aggregate authorized capital was 5.3 percent as of January 1, 2000, 4.8 percent as of January 1, 2001, 4.1 percent as of January 1, 2002, 3.1 percent as of January 1, 2003 and 2.7 percent as of January 1, 2004.

with a view to enhancing public information and awareness—and *consumer protection* rules, which appear to be currently absent in the Russian Federation. To this purpose, legal protection of policyholders should operate at least at two levels:

— *Contractual level:* by means of new legal rules aimed, *inter alia*, at monitoring unfair terms in consumer contracts,[20] providing guidance in the interpretation of standard forms, establishing non-waivable consumers' rights of cancellation, withdrawal, information, and so forth.
— *Enforcement level:* by means of new legal rules aimed, *inter alia*, at governing claims handling practices, introducing alternative dispute resolution mechanisms, and so forth. In case of non-compliance, licenses will be revoked.

Regulatory and Supervisory Framework

Following the establishment of the Federal Insurance Supervision Service (FISS) in March 2004, FISS is in charge of insurance supervision and control, while the regulation of the insurance market remains the responsibility of the Ministry of Finance. Procedures have been established for close coordination between MOF and FISS. The new insurance regulator is organized in four directorates, with a central inspectorate located in Moscow[21] and several regional inspection units. Even is the number of staff in charge of on-site and off-site controls have been increased, it is impossible for the FISS to effectively monitor 1397 insurance companies. A top priority is the in order to drastically reduce the number of players. This would also lead to an increase in transparency and in the overall quality of the market players since, reportedly, several of the smallest companies are only offering tax optimization schemes, such as wage schemes. According to the FISS, moreover, the 50 top companies already account for 60 to 70 percent of gross written premiums and of shareholder capital.

The new FISS is not financially independent from the Ministry of Finance and the budget currently allocated is not sufficient to provide the amount of human and technical resources needed to effectively perform the supervisory tasks. Excessively long licensing procedures and the lack of sufficient staff have been reported as examples of the problem. Moreover, the low level of FISS salaries, as compared to private sector opportunities for qualified professionals, generates a high turnover of staff and the need for continuous re-training. The Head of the supervisory body recognizes these impediments, but the only way out that he currently envisages is relying on funds provided by the EU TACIS Program. To this purpose, the insurance supervisory authority should be established as an agency outside Federal budget and a levy imposed on supervised entities should be considered as source of funding; this would allow the agency to escape Federal salary caps, increase its political independence and reduce incentives for corruption.

---

20. See Directive 1993/13/EEC.
21. It shall be noted that the central district accounts for 80 percent of the market.

Power to Apply Fit and Proper Tests for Controllers and Significant Owners of Insurance Companies

According to the 2002 "Concept of Insurance Market Development in the Russian Federation" (Decree n. 1361-p, see *supra*), the scope of government supervision should also include:

— the assessment of the good standing of the promoters (shareholders, members, affiliated persons and beneficial owners) and their shares in the authorized capital of an insurance company; and
— the establishment of procedures for financial recovery, reorganization and, eventually, liquidation of the insurance undertakings.

Unfortunately, these two crucial aspects have not been fully addressed in the approved amending law of 2003 (Federal Law n.172-FZ of December 10, 2003). In fact, even if insurers must submit to the authority information about their direct shareholders, including data on their affiliated foreign investors, no fit and proper test has been introduced with reference to shareholders and other parties having a direct or indirect interest in the insurance undertaking; moreover, the supervisory authority has not been entrusted with the power to monitor and approve/refuse the acquisition and/or transfer of qualifying holdings in insurance undertakings (changes of control), nor to check the source of the funds used to acquire control of an insurance company.

The IAIS Guidance Paper for Fit and Proper Principles and their Application[22] clearly states that in order to assist in ensuring that supervised entities are operated prudently and soundly, fitness and propriety or other qualification tests should be applied not only to directors and managers, but also to shareholders and other persons exercising a material and controlling influence on the management, operations or shareholdings of supervised insurance entities ("controllers"). The same requirement is set forth by IAIS Insurance Core Principle 7 (*Suitability of persons*): "The significant owners, board members, senior management, auditors and actuaries of an insurer are fit and proper to fulfill their roles. This requires that they possess the appropriate integrity, competency, experience and qualification."[23] A significant owner is defined as a person (legal or natural) that directly or indirectly, alone or with an associate, exercises control over the insurer[24].

The fact that the FISS lacks the power to check the suitability of "controllers" and "significant owners" of insurance undertakings is particularly problematic in the Russian Federation, since it hinders the possibility for the supervisor to conduct an effective scrutiny aimed at preventing imprudent or unsound management of insurance companies, opaque financial practices, money laundering, and other illegal uses of the insurance and reinsurance markets.

---

22. IAIS—Insurance Fraud Subcommittee, Guidance Paper for Fit and Proper Principles and their Application, approved in Cape Town on 10th October 2000.

23. *See:* IAIS Insurance Core Principles and Methodology, October 2003.

24. Pursuant to IAIS ICP 8 EC (a) the term "control" over an insurer is defined in legislation and it addresses: (i) holding of a defined number or percentage of issued shares or specified financial instruments (such as compulsory convertible debentures) above a designated threshold in an insurer or its intermediate or ultimate beneficial owner; (ii) voting rights attached to the aforementioned shares or financial instruments; (iii) power to appoint or remove directors to the board or other executive committees.

Power to Apply Safeguards and Sanctions

More generally, the supervisory authority should be able to introduce appropriate safeguards or impose sanctions aimed at preventing irregularities and infringements of the provisions on insurance supervision.[25] The authority should be entitled to take at least the following resolution measures against those insurance companies which do not adhere to the law and to the regulations: impose obligation on a violator to take adequate measures and remove the violation; require convening an extraordinary shareholders' meeting; impose fines for non-compliance; dismiss the management and appoint its provisional administration; adopt the financial recovery plan to reestablish financial stability of an insurance undertaking; motion liquidation of an insolvent insurance company. In order to provide adequate incentives to fulfill supervisory duties, a certain degree of immunity and legal protection should be granted to FISS and its staff, for all actions taken in good faith and without negligence.

Relations with External Auditors

The role of external auditors should also be improved in the monitoring of the financial condition of supervised insurance companies: in the course of performance of their duties, auditors should be required to report immediately to the FISS in case they discover anything that may constitute a threat to the solvency of an insurance company. To this purpose, the FISS should establish a closer relationship with the auditors of insurance companies.

Supervision of Financial Conglomerates

Another relevant concern is the current lack of specific rules on supplemental supervision for insurance companies belonging to an insurance group or to a financial conglomerate. In the harmonized EC legislation, special provisions are devoted to the tackle problems related to double gearing, capital leverage[26] and intra-group transactions that may have a negative influence in the solvency situation of insurance undertakings. Directive 2002/87/EC, moreover, lays down new rules for supplementary supervision of regulated entities which are part of a financial conglomerate: according to the Directive, prudential supervision shall be conducted on a group-wide basis, in particular as regards the solvency position and risk concentration at the level of the conglomerate, the intra-group transactions, and the internal risk management processes at conglomerate level.[27] The FISS should also consider entering into Memoranda of Understanding with foreign counterparts in order to achieve the required coordination.

In light of the above, the FISS should consider the opportunity to coordinate with other Federal Agencies or Services in the supervision of financial conglomerates, establishing standard practices and clarifying the respective roles.[28]

---

25. See IAIS ICP 14 and 15 (October, 2003).

26. The risk is that holding companies may become excessively indebted and try to withdraw capital from their insurance subsidiaries, in order to reimburse their debts.

27. See also: IAIS ICP17 (group-wide supervision) (October, 2003).

28. In those countries, such as the Russian Federation, that do not have opted for a single financial supervisory authority, the supervision of financial conglomerates can be conducted by way of co-operation agreements among the various authorities, with one of them acting as *lead supervisor*.

Supervision of Reinsurance Activities

Current reinsurance practices deserve special attention, especially in light of the fact that a substantial amount of outgoing reinsurance does not appear to be directed towards well-established reinsurance markets. The FISS should be granted express powers to effectively monitor and review the reinsurance programs of supervised entities, to assess the quality of domestic and foreign reinsures, and to mandate changes when required. Along these lines, the FISS may consider the opportunity to stipulate information sharing agreements and Memoranda of Understanding[29] with foreign authorities in order to be able to acquire confidential information on cross border insurance and reinsurance operations, also for the purpose of preventing money laundering and other illegal activities.[30]

Supervision of Corporate Governance and Internal Controls

Another area of the insurance supervision that needs to be improved is that of corporate governance and internal controls.[31] A system of internal control is critical to effective risk management and a foundation for the safe and sound operation of an insurer. It provides a systematic and disciplined approach to evaluating and improving the effectiveness of the operation and assuring compliance with laws and regulations. At present, insurance companies in Russia do not have an internal control (audit) function and the supervisor has no power to require and verify that the insurer complies with applicable corporate governance principles.

Strictly related to the above mentioned lack of effective internal control functions is the need to strengthen the current regulation and supervision of the investment activities of insurance undertakings, in order to ensure full compliance with best practices and international standards.[32] The supervisory authority must require insurers to comply with standards on investment activities, including requirements on investment policy, asset mix, valuation, diversification, asset-liability matching, and risk management. At present, according to some sources, several insurance companies engage in extensive trading in high risk shares and volatile financial instruments, and modify the composition of their investment portfolio only at the time of the annual reporting, in order to dissimulate full compliance with the required spread and diversification rules. The changes in the investment portfolio of insurance companies should be more closely monitored through more frequent and detailed reporting requirements, electronic reporting, on site inspections, and the establishment of an independent internal audit function.

Transparency of FISS Decisions

In order to make FISS's decision making process publicly perceived as transparent and accountable, information about the role, procedures and activities of the FISS should be

---

29. See IAIS ICP5 (October, 2003).
30. See also: IAIS Guidance Paper n.5, Anti-Money Laundering Guidance Notes for Insurance Supervisors and Insurance Entities (Approved, January 2002).
31. See IAIS ICP 9 and 10 (October, 2003).
32. See e.g. IAIS ICP 21 (October, 2003).

made publicly available, together with detailed information about the evolution of the insurance market in general. The supervisory authority should publish in an annual report a summary its activities, objectives, financial situation of the supervised companies, market trends and concerns, key vulnerabilities and other relevant information. In addition to these reports, the FISS should keep the public constantly informed through press conferences and seminars. As mentioned, moreover, transparency and accountability can be ensured by requiring a detailed rationale for every decision, and by allowing for some degree of judicial review of the decisions made by the supervisory body. In any event, the issue appears to be one of crucial importance for the healthy and ordered growth of the Russian insurance market.

Key Priorities Going Forward

In light of the above, key policy reform priorities for the development of the insurance sector are as follows:

(i) Improve compliance with IAIS principles.
(ii) Establish FISS as an independent agency with its own funding sources. The FISS currently does not have enough human and technical resources to properly fulfill its supervisory duties. The salary of staff is extremely low as compared to private sector alternatives and this generates a high turnover with the consequence the FISS may seriously suffer from a lack of qualified professionals. The insurance supervisory authority should be established as an agency outside Federal budget and a levy imposed on supervised entities should be considered as source of funding; this would allow the agency to escape Federal salary caps, increase its political independence and reduce incentives for corruption.
(iii) Strengthen coordination between FISS and the Ministry of Finance. The Russian Federation opted for a separation of the supervisory functions (Federal Insurance Supervision Service) from the regulatory functions (Ministry of Finance): this requires proper coordination in order to avoid malfunctioning of the system. In particular, coordination efforts should focus on the re-draft of the rules concerning reporting standards, the formation of technical reserves and the investment of assets covering them. The re-unification of the two functions in a fully independent authority should also be considered in the long run.
(iv) Strictly enforce increased minimum capital requirements and conduct re-licensing of all existing insurance companies. The FISS should devote special attention to this crucial step, since it has the potential to rule out of the market several small and undercapitalized companies exclusively involved in tax schemes. Moreover, a substantial reduction in the number of insurers will make supervision more manageable and will enhance the quality and reputation of the market participants. Taking the occasion of the enforcement of these new capital requirements, and of the mandatory separation between life and non-life businesses, the FISS should undertake a comprehensive re-licensing of existing insurance companies.

(v) Grant to FISS should the power to check the fitness and propriety of qualified shareholders, controllers and beneficial owners of the insurance companies at the licensing/re-licensing stage, as well as to approve subsequent changes in control of supervised entities.

(vi) Strengthen monitoring of investment activities and changes in the investment portfolio of insurance undertakings by FISS in order to prevent excessive risk taking. To this purpose, more frequent and detailed reporting is highly advisable and the authority should also improve coordination with external auditors.

(vii) Establish clear anti-money laundering procedures should be established and strictly enforced in the insurance sector, especially for those companies involved in life insurance. Specific references can be found in the IAIS *Anti-Money Laundering Guidance Notes for Insurance Supervisors and Insurance Entities* (2002). Training of insurance professionals in this area is particularly important and representatives of ARIA (All Russian Insurance Association) ranked this among the top industry priorities.

(viii) Establish rules on supplemental supervision for insurance companies belonging to an insurance group or a financial conglomerate should be introduced. Supplemental supervision is aimed at tackling problems related to double gearing, capital leverage and intra-group transactions that may have a negative influence in the solvency situation of insurance undertakings. Considering the number of captive insurance companies actively operating in Russia this issue deserves special attention. Until special provisions are introduced, the FISS should consider the opportunity to coordinate with other Federal Agencies or Services in the supervision of financial conglomerates, establishing standard practices and clarifying the respective roles. The FISS should also consider entering into Memoranda of Understanding with foreign counterparts in order to achieve the required coordination.

(ix) Grant to FISS the power to review the reinsurance policy of supervised entities and to mandate changes if needed. The authority should also consider the opportunity to enter into Memoranda of Understanding and/or information sharing agreements with foreign supervisors, in order to obtain confidential information about foreign reinsures.

(x) Grant to FISS the power to intervene early in case of threat to the solvency of an insurance undertaking and to impose urgent measures for crisis management and financial recovery.

(xi) Strengthen the role of FISS in the liquidation process should be clarified and the claims of policyholders should be granted a degree of priority over those of the other creditors.

(xii) Require insurance companies to have an internal control (audit) function and the FISS should be in a position to require and verify that the insurer complies with applicable corporate governance principles.

(xiii) Enact consumer protection rules to stimulate the growth of the voluntary retail market. The protection of policyholders should focus on both the contractual level (contractual terms and conditions of coverage) and on the enforcement level (claims handling practices, alternative dispute resolution mechanisms, etc.).

To this purpose, special attention should also be devoted the monitoring of professional qualification of insurance intermediaries (brokers and agents), all of which should be supervised by the FISS.[33] Clear guidance in this direction can be found in Directive 2002/92/EC on insurance mediation.

(xiv) Revise current rules on compulsory MTPL with a view to increasing flexibility with regard to both claims handling (with the introduction of "amicable settlement forms") and contractual terms ("bonus/malus," flex-time coverages, and so forth). Moreover, tariffs should be set on the basis of sound actuarial calculations, and not merely as a result of a political decision.

(xv) Establish requirements for types and structure of investment assets for insurance companies. (Eligible financial instruments, limits; the investment rules should based on market mechanisms and risk profile of insurance companies).

---

33. Currently, only brokers are subject to supervision.

The Capital Market Development Project[1]

Project Background

To regulate the emerging securities industry, in November 1994, GOR established a new federal agency—the Federal Commission for the Securities Market (FCSM). In March 1995, the FCSM was given ministerial status and the mandate to develop, implement and enforce regulations governing the activities of professional market participants.

In May 1996, the Bank's Board approved CMDP, which was originally designed to support the second stage of GOR's capital market's development program. Following completion of the first stage (mass privatization), the second stage of the program was to focus on building a sustainable capital market integrated with the wider financial system. The project had three key components: (i) a regulatory infrastructure component which was to establish the policy framework, laws and regulations and the institutional capacity in regulation and self-regulation which constitute the essential underpinning of modern capital markets; (ii) a market architecture component which was to support private sector organizations in building efficient, fair and secure trading, clearance, settlement and registrations systems, and (iii) a Government Securities Tracking System which was to enhance the capability of the Ministry of Finance to manage Government debt.

Following the 1998 crisis, which severely impacted the financial sector, GOR and the Bank carried out a joint assessment to identify key priorities going forward. While the overall project development objectives remained valid, the project was restructured to address acute, near-term needs for development of the market. Although they remain

---

1. Extract from project supervision mission Aide-Memoire 12/05.

important for efficient market development, the components related to the development of the physical market architecture were dropped in view of their relatively sound state of development. Focus was placed instead on major constraints to market development in the area of corporate governance and effective regulation. To reflect the narrower scope of the Project going forward, the Loan size, which originally amounted to $89 million, was reduced to $55.25 million. In addition, to allow for completion of Project activities, which were delayed as a result of various circumstances ranging from disruptions following the 1998 crisis to procurement delays and inadequate authorized federal budget funding for the Commission, the Project was extended twice in 2000 and 2002 at the request of the MOF.

In March 2004, GOR carried out a comprehensive administrative reform. The former Securities Market Regulator (the FCSM) was abolished and a new regulator (the Federal Financial Markets Service—FFMS) was created in its place. The FFMS inherited the monitoring, supervisory and regulatory functions of the FCSM. In addition, its mandate was broadened to include legal and regulatory responsibilities over all segments of the financial market with the exception of banking (CBR), insurance (Federal Insurance Supervision Service), and audit (MOF).

The FFMS was recognized as the legal successor of the FCSM for the purpose of CMDP. In August 2004, the MOF thus requested an additional two-year Project extension to complete several key components (delayed in part as a result of the Government reorganization) and implement complementary activities in line with the Project Development Objectives. Accordingly, in September 2004, the Bank extended CMDP through December 31, 2006. The loan amount was also further reduced to $54.91 million.

As of December 1, 2005, $40.491 million had been disbursed and $14.419 million remain undisbursed, of which $3.615 million are committed under signed contracts. New contracts in the amount of $4.610 million are about to be signed and $4.167 million are currently being negotiated. The Project is rated Satisfactory by the Bank.

Project Contribution to Capital Markets Development and Policy Agenda to Date

Despite a slow resumption of Project activities following the 1998 crisis restructuring, CMDP's overall contribution to the reform agenda in securities market regulation and supervision has been noteworthy.

The Legal support component resulted in significant improvements in the legal framework for protection of investors' rights including the Joint-Stock Company Law, the Securities Market Law and the Law on Investment Funds. Adopted provisions have been important in stemming two of the most common corporate governance abuses—asset-stripping where company assets were sold at below-market prices to related parties and share-dilution where new share issuances forcibly diluted the percentage ownership of existing shareholders.

The Enforcement component strengthened the enforcement capacity of the Regulator. Detailed customized operational guidelines on how to detect and investigate market offenses were developed; various enforcement agencies involved in securities market oversight and supervision were trained and investor education materials informing investors of their rights and recourse were developed. Under the Information and Public Relations component, the Commission's Internet site was redesigned and improved with a view to facilitating investor access to important material information and strengthening the transparency and accountability of the Regulator. Finally, the Accounting and Disclosure components helped strengthen transparency of company reporting. Russian information disclosure standards were also brought in closer line with international standards and new mechanisms providing for easy, timely and low cost access to information disclosed by Russian public companies were introduced.

In addition, following the March 2004 Government's reorganization, the Loan continued to finance the Group of technical experts providing policy, economic advice and legal drafting assistance to the FFMS. Key contributions over the past two years include:

- Development of the FFMS Financial Market Development Strategy (expected to be adopted by GOR in February 2006);
- Introduction of stricter listing and trade reporting requirements for Exchanges and market participants in closer line with international standards;
- Development and adoption of secondary legislation to complete the legal base for mortgage-backed securities;
- Introduction of legal provisions to improve regulation of the pension funds industry in relation to investment of second pillar mandatory pension funds;
- Development of legal provisions to the Securities Market Law and the Joint-Stock Company Law to improve the legal framework for domestic IPOs (expected to be adopted in early 2006);
- Amendments to the Securities Market Law to establish a legal base for short-term corporate bonds equivalent to commercial papers (expected to be adopted in 2006);
- Amendments to the Securities Market Law to enable issuance and trading of Russian Depositary Receipts on foreign stocks on domestic exchanges (expected to be adopted in 2006).

Recent Market Developments and Remaining Agenda

Russian securities markets and institutional investors have undergone remarkable development and growth in recent years.

On the supply side, the market grew significantly not only as a result of price appreciation of outstanding securities, but also as a result of new placements of Russian securities both on domestic and international markets. Equity market capitalization expanded rapidly from its 1.2 trillion rubles 2000 basis (17 percent of GDP) to about 6.9 trillion rubles (or 41 percent of GDP) by end 2004. In 2005, new companies admitted for trading as a result of energy sector reforms along with the surge in price of blue chips (primarily Gazprom) led to a new unprecedented growth, raising market capitalization to an estimated 60 percent of GDP. The number of Russian IPOs is also growing both on domestic and international markets and is expanding beyond the traditional large extractive industry and energy sector corporate issuers to include smaller retail, pharmaceutical and internet/media companies. The domestic corporate bond market has also undergone substantial development both in size and quality and is becoming an important source of financing for mid and large corporate issuers in various industries with a noticeable lengthening of average maturity (four year duration for 2005 bond placements).

On the demand side, the role of domestic and foreign institutional investors is growing. The investor base on the equity market includes a greater share of global investment funds with longer-term investment strategies. On the domestic bond market side, domestic pension funds and investment funds as well as asset management companies have also begun to play a more visible role.

Despite the above recent positive developments, some important market weaknesses and impediments remain. On the supply side, the equity market remains largely concentrated among few issuers in terms of capitalization, free-float, and turnover. The high transaction cost and risk of domestic trading, along with continuing perceptions of poor protection of investors' rights, have tended to drive secondary trading abroad (primarily to the London market). Derivatives' trading is limited due to the absence of a solid legal base and protection of derivatives transactions. On the demand side, while the role of domestic institutional investors (investment funds, pension funds, and insurance companies) has been growing, it remains marginal in comparison with other type of investors. The settlement and clearing infrastructure remains fragmented and full DVP (Delivery vs. payment) clearing with guaranteed execution of trading is not available on domestic exchange platforms.

To bring the domestic market up to international standards and make it competitive in comparison with major international securities exchanges, a number of legal, regulatory and infrastructure issues remain to be addressed. Required improvements include *inter alia* the introduction and enforcement of effective rules against insider trading and price manipulation; introduction of legal protection for derivatives transactions; and introduction of a centralized clearing and settlement system to streamline securities trading and reduce transaction cost and risk.

Additional loan activities agreed during Loan extension discussions in the fall of 2004 will help address these issues and strengthen the institutional capacity of the Regulator. These activities include:

- The establishment of a Central Depositary;
- Strengthening of the FFMS monitoring and supervision powers over market participants, including prudential supervision to enhance market transparency, minimize existing market risks and protect investor's rights; and
- Enhancement of corporate governance particularly in the area of corporate management fiduciary duties and use of insider information.

These activities which are currently under way as well as the continued work of the group of technical experts financed under the Loan are expected to complete the foundation built to date in the area of legal drafting, market infrastructure development, prudential supervision and protection of investors' rights.

Status of Project Activities

Central Depositary: The objective of the Central Depository activity (CD) is to develop a Centralized Clearing and Settlement system to help reduce transaction cost and risks related to securities trading and registration—thereby bringing up the level of Russian securities trading infrastructure to international standards and increasing trust in domestic securities trading. The assignment is expected to be performed in three stages: (i) analysis of the existing market infrastructure, review of foreign experience in CSS, and development of an operational model and plan for establishment of a CD; (ii) development of a draft Federal Law regulating the status and functions of the CD and; (iii) Development of draft regulations on the rules of interaction of the CD with other market infrastructure institutions (registrars, depositories, clearing organizations, trading floors). Contract amount: $2 million. Contract signed on January 9, 2006. Duration of the assignment: 9 months.

Prudential Supervision: The objective of the Prudential Supervision activity is to strengthen FFMS's monitoring and supervision powers over financial market participants to enhance market reliability and stability and increase protection of investors' rights and interests. The enhanced prudential supervision framework to be developed under this component is expected to include appropriate sanctions for non-compliance. The Prudential supervision activity will consist of three stages: (i) Risk analysis on the Russian financial market; (ii) Development of a monitoring and market surveillance system; (iii) Drafting of new laws and regulations and amendments to existing legal acts regulating the securities market to allow for introduction of new prudential supervision norms. Contract amount: $395,000. Contract signed on November 2, 2005. Duration of the assignment: 6 months.

Corporate Governance: The objective of the Corporate Governance activity is to enhance investor confidence in the Russian financial market, encourage good faith performance of duties by company officials in the interest of the company and its shareholders and introduce mechanisms preventing use of insider information and market manipulation. The Assignment is expected to consist of two stages: (i) comparative analysis of Russian and foreign experience in the area of legal regulation and judicial practice in respect of board members' fiduciary responsibilities, grounds for civil, administrative and criminal liability for improper performance of duties and abuse of company shareholders' interests; (ii) Drafting of legal provisions establishing mechanisms for holding company officials liable including development of the Federal Law on insider information and market manipulation. Contract amount: $993,000. Contract expected to be signed by mid-end January 2006. Duration of the assignment: 8 months.

Development of the ITA Architecture of the FFMS (overall: $9.49 million): The IT architecture of the Regulator envisaged three modules: (i) hardware, (ii) telecommunications facilities, and (iii) software components. Most of the server equipment, workstations and telecommunications systems under module 1 and 2 have been delivered. The third module (the software component) which is designed to support the Regulator's key business functions (including Joint Stock Companies registration, licensing of market participants, certification, information disclosure and market monitoring) is currently being tendered out. Due to its technical complexity, this component has experienced severe delays in conjunction with the formulation of the required technical specifications and technical evaluation of bidder proposals. Given the limited time left under the Loan and the extended estimated length of the assignment (14 months), the Commission is concerned that the envisioned task may not be feasible within the remaining life period of the Project and, thus, that it may be more realistic to reconsider the current scope of work and possibly organize a new tender to procure a smaller portion of the expected packages of goods and services, with the balance to be financed by the budget the Russian Federation at a later stage. Contract amount: $4.17 million.

Government Debt Management ($4.00 million): This component envisages technical support for development of analytical and risk management tools and the creation of a unified State Debt Information System. In November 2004, the MOF developed a detailed timetable of activities including: (i) legislative drafting establishing different levels of liability (direct, contingent), allowing open market operations and introducing the concept of performance-based budgeting; (ii) software development and training, and (iii) equipment procurement. In May 2005, the MOF expressed its interest in raising the level of co-financing from the Russian budget and decrease the share of Bank Loan financing to a minimum. However, official communication to this effect has not yet been received by the Bank. During the Bank's December 2005 supervision mission, the MOF noted that, in view of the recent favorable macroeconomic situation which has allowed the Russian Federation to restructure its external debt and decrease its ratio to GDP to 12 percent, the needs and task as originally envisioned under this component may need to be reformulated. The MOF indicated that it would communicate its final decision to the Bank with regards to the use of the Debt component by early February 2006.

Individual Consultants Group ($4.33 million): CMDP is steered by a group of 12 technical experts in the area of legal drafting, collective investment funds, information disclosure and public relations, macroeconomic factors impacting securities markets, information technology, prudential supervision and professional training and monitoring of risks on financial markets. This group has played an essential role in the development and implementation of the Project components and has been a precious intellectual resource to the Commission. A detailed description of their ongoing activities and contribution to the policy agenda is attached to this Aide Memoire.

Issues and Next Steps

Status of steps identified during the Bank's September 2005 supervision mission:

- CCMD to complete tender process for Central Depository component and sign contract with winning bidder by end September, 2005: *completed.*
- CCMD to complete tender process for Corporate Governance and sign contract with winning bidder by end November 2005: *completed.*
- CCMD to send results of technical evaluation for the IT software component by end September 2005: *completed; however, final result of the tender still pending.*
- FFMS to inform the Bank on Government decision regarding the Single Regulator component by mid December 2005: *completed. It was decided that this issue would not be addressed under the Loan and that a portion of the amount earmarked for this activity would be reallocated instead to the Central Depository component.*

New issues and next steps to be addressed by March 2006:

■ CCMD and FFMS to complete the IT Software component procurement process and communicate results of negotiations to the Bank by end-January, 2006.
■ MOF to communicate its final decision regarding the Debt Component to the Bank by mid-February, 2006.
■ MOF, FFMS, and CCMD to take stock of Loan disbursement progress and identify Loan amounts unlikely to be disbursed within the life of the Project and send official request to the Bank for cancellation of corresponding amounts by March 1, 2006.

Table 21: Technical Advisors Activities and Contribution to Policy Agenda (2004–05 Results)

Final Output (Concept Notes, Draft Laws, Draft Normative Acts, etc.)	Capital Market Issues Covered	Status as of End 2004	Status as of End 2005
1. Capital Market Development Strategy—Improving Effectiveness of Market Regulation			
Draft Financial Market Development Strategy	Outlines key impediments, provides recommendations to address existing impediments and sets mid-term development goals. Strategy covers: ■ Improvements to investment rules for management of the funded portion of the mandatory pension system (Second pillar); ■ New forms of voluntary pension savings (Third pillar); ■ Unified standards of investment activities of collective investments' institutions; ■ Improvement in operation of exchanges and trading systems; ■ Establishment of legal base for new types of financial instruments; ■ Protection of share-holder's rights in mergers, acquisition and reorganization.		Submitted to GOR—expected to be approved in Feb. 2006

(continued)

**Table 21: Technical Advisors Activities and Contribution to Policy Agenda
(2004–05 Results) (*Continued*)**

Final Output (Concept Notes, Draft Laws, Draft Normative Acts, etc.)	Capital Market Issues Covered	Status as of End 2004	Status as of End 2005
2. Securities Market Infrastructure Development and Supervision of Professional Market Participants Activities			
FFMS Regulation on activities related to the organization of securities trading	Sets requirements for stock exchanges, rules for securities admission to exchange trading, listing requirements, rules on forward transactions on stock exchanges.	Enacted	
Amendments to FFMS Regulation on activities related to the organization of securities trading	Sets requirements for market participants to report results of trade execution, special requirements for listing of securities issued in the process of re-organization.		Enacted
Draft Amendments to FFMS Regulation on activities related to the organization of securities trading	Sets special listing requirements for IPOs and new rules for forward transactions on stock exchanges.		In the Ministry of Justice
FFMS order on approval of licensing rules for various types of professional market participants	Sets FFMS rules for licensing of professional market participants.		Enacted
Concept of the Draft Law on Central Depositary	Establishes foundation for the centralized securities settlement system.		Adopted by GOR
3. Introduction and Development of New Financial Instruments			
Draft Federal Law on amendments to the Securities Market Law and other legal acts to set rules for issuance and trading of short-term bonds (commercial paper)	Sets procedures for issuance and trading of short-term bonds (equivalent to commercial papers) using simplified procedures (no state registration of issuance reports and results of issuance required).		
Draft Federal Law on amendments to the Securities Market Law to enable domestic issuance and trading of Russian Depositary Receipts on foreign stocks	Sets procedures for issuance and trading of Russian.Depositary Receipts (RDR) on foreign stocks; sets rights and obligations of depositaries, foreign security issuers and RDR investors		Being cleared by Legal Directory of the President

Table 21: Technical Advisors Activities and Contribution to Policy Agenda (2004–05 Results) (*Continued*)

Final Output (Concept Notes, Draft Laws, Draft Normative Acts, etc.)	Capital Market Issues Covered	Status as of End 2004	Status as of End 2005
Amendments to legislation in the area of assets securitization	Develops legal base for new financial instruments created for the purpose of refinancing assets of legal entities (introduction of collateral rights on bank accounts, rules for SPV activities, introduction of procedures for general shareholders meeting, introduction of escrow accounts, etc.)		In the process of drafting
Draft Amendment to Civil Code Article (1062) related tolegal protection of derivatives transactions	Extends legal protection for derivative transactions (According to the current version of the Civil Code, derivative transactions are legally equivalent to gam-bling transactions which are not protected by the law).		Sent to State Duma for discussion
Amendments to the Law on Insolvency (Bankruptcy) and Article 50–20 of the Federal Law On the Insolvency (bankruptcy) of Credit Institutions	Establishes "liquidation netting" procedures for derivatives transactions (protects securities transactions from non-execution of trade in case of bankruptcy)		In the process of drafting
Amendments to several legal acts to streamline securities market legislation in accordance with the Federal Law on Mortgage Backed Securities	Introduces amendments to securities market legislation to remove legal impediments to issuance of mortgage-backed securities.	Encted	
FFMS Order on rules defining the size of mortgage collateral	Defines the rules for valuation of assets that are used for loan coverage by mortgage.		Enacted
FFMS Order on the activities of special depositary related to mortgage collateral	Sets requirements for the activities of special depositaries, including supervision functions and maintenance of mortgage registry.		Enacted

4. Development of Collective Investment Institutions and Pension Reform (Institutional Investments and Pension Reform)

4.1. Regulation of Investment Funds

Regulations on activities of asset management companies for Joint Stock Investment Funds (corporate investment funds) and Unit Investment Funds (contractual investment funds)	Prohibits the use of historical price for calculation of investment funds' NAV, prohibits price manipulation, develops internal control mechanism for asset management companies.	Enacted	

(*continued*)

Table 21: Technical Advisors Activities and Contribution to Policy Agenda (2004–05 Results) (*Continued*)

Final Output (Concept Notes, Draft Laws, Draft Normative Acts, etc.)	Capital Market Issues Covered	Status as of End 2004	Status as of End 2005
Regulation of activities of special depositaries for corporate and contractual investment funds, as well as non-state pension funds (NSPF)	Sets requirements for special depositaries of corporate investment funds, unit investment funds, private pension funds, including monitoring functions of special depositaries over assets of funds held by depositaries.	Enacted	
Regulation on the structure and types of assets allowed for corporate and contractual investment funds	Sets requirements on the structure and type of allowed investments for corporate and unit investment funds.		Enacted
Regulation on procedures used for calculation of the NAV for corporate and contractual investment funds	Sets NAV calculation (including NAV per share) rules for corporate and contractual investment funds.		Enacted
Regulation on information disclosure for corporate investment funds and asset management companies of contractual investment funds	Introduces more effective information disclosure, cost reduction through internet-based information disclosure, information disclosure standards for corporate investment funds and asset management companies of contractual investment funds.		Enacted
4.2. Regulation of Investments of the Funded Portion of the Mandatory Pension System (Second pillar)			
Methodology for selection of special depositary (SD) for the state pension fund (SPF) of Russia	Establishes normative base for investment of the Second pillar; sets clear and transparent criteria for the selection of SD for SPF		Enacted
Regulation on reporting requirements for the SPF in relation to the accumulation and investment of second pillar funds	mproves transparency of Second pillar funds managed by the SPF.		Enacted
Reporting standards for the Special Depositary of the SPF	Sets FFMS reporting requirements for the Special Depositary of the SPF		Enacted
Reporting standards for the State Asset Management Company (State AMC)	Sets FFMS reporting standards for the State AMC managing second pillar funds of the SPF.		Enacted

**Table 21: Technical Advisors Activities and Contribution to Policy Agenda
(2004–05 Results) (*Continued*)**

Final Output (Concept Notes, Draft Laws, Draft Normative Acts, etc.)	Capital Market Issues Covered	Status as of End 2004	Status as of End 2005130
4.3. Regulation of Non-State Pension Funds (NSPF) In relation to both pillar 2 (accumulative portion of the mandatory pension) and pillar 3 (voluntary pension coverage)			
Draft amendment to government regulation on authority and responsibility of the federal executive body responsible for regulation of private pension funds' activities related to investments of pillar 2 funds	Defines the authority of the FFMS and the Ministry of Health and Social Development in relation to monitoring, regulation and supervision of NSPFs		Introduced to GOR
Reporting standards for private pension funds in relation to Second pillar funds	Sets reporting requirements for the SD to ensure effective supervision.		Enacted
Procedures for calculation of market value and NAV of pension assets managed by NSPF	Establishes unified requirements for market valuation of pension assets.		Enacted
5. Information Disclosure on Financial Markets/Mechanism for Improved Corporate Governance			
Concept of the federal law on inside information and price manipulation on financial markets	Proposes mechanisms to make Russian legislation more effective in preventing unfair market practices (insider trading and price manipulation).		Sent to GOR
Draft amendments to the Securities Market Law, the Joint Stock Company Law, the Investor Rights Protection Law	Improving the legal base for IPOs.		Approved by duma and federation council
Improved standards and procedures for security issuance and prospects registration	New requirements for calculation of initial placement price, improved issuance procedures during reorganization of JSC, improved forms of registration of new securities.		Approved by FFMS Order and effective
Draft Federal Law amending the JSC law and other legislation in relation to merger procedures	Improves regulation of mergers and acquisition, establishes more specific procedures and strengthens protection of shareholders' rights.		Passed 2nd Duma reading

(*continued*)

**Table 21: Technical Advisors Activities and Contribution to Policy Agenda
(2004–05 Results) (*Continued*)**

Final Output (Concept Notes, Draft Laws, Draft Normative Acts, etc.)	Capital Market Issues Covered	Status as of End 2004	Status as of End 2005
6. Developing Liability and Responsibilities (Fiduciary duties) for Financial Market Participants			
Draft amendments to the code of administrative violations	To introduce liability for violation of the Investment Fund Law, increase sanctions for violation of Securities Market Law and Law on Joint Stock Companies, improve enforcement mechanisms of administrative penalties on the securities market.		Sent to GOR
Draft amendments to the Criminal Code and Criminal Procedural Code	Increase liability for violations of securities market laws and regulations.		Sent to GOR

Bibliography

All Russian Insurance Association. Official website.

Bureau of Economic Analysis Bulletin, No. 50, December 2003.

Cbonds information agency. Official website: www.cbonds.ru.

    Cbonds monthly bulletin on municipal bonds

    Cbonds monthly bulletin on corporate bonds

    Cbonds monthly bulleting on eurobonds

Central Bank of Russia. *Bulletin of Banking Statistics 2003.*

————. *Bulletin of Banking Statistics 2004.*

————. *Bulletin of Banking Statistics 2005.*

————. *Banking Supervision Report 2003.*

————. *Banking Supervision Report 2004.*

————. Official website: www.cbr.ru

    Government Bonds Database

    Statistical Section

Emerging Markets Database.

Federal Financial Insurance Service. Official website.

Federal Financial Market Service. *The draft mid-term strategy for financial market development (2005–2008).*

————. *The mid-term strategy for financial market development (2006–2008).*

————. Website: www.fcsm.ru

    Market Participants Section

    SRO Section

    Legal Section

    Pension Reform Section

    Corporate Governance Section

International Monetary Fund. *International Financial Statistics* Database.

Ministry of Finance of the Russian Federation. Official website: www.minfin.ru.

    External Debt Section

    Domestic Debt Section

National League of Asset Managers. Official website: www.nlu.ru.

Pension Fund of Russia. Official website.

Renaissance Capital Equity Handbook 2003, 2004, 2005. www.rencap.ru.

Rusbonds. Official website: www.rusbonds.ru.

State Asset Management Company (Vnesheconom bank). Official website.

Troika Dialog. Fixed Income Overview 2003, 2004, 2005. www.troika.ru

World Bank. Russian Capital Market Database. Built for the NBFI study, IBRD Moscow.

————. Russian Macroeconomic Data Database. Built by PREM department, IBRD Moscow.

Other Websites

www.gks.ru
www.micex.ru
www.naufor.ru
www.rts.ru

www.ingramcontent.com/pod-product-compliance
Lightning Source LLC
Chambersburg PA
CBHW080333270326
41927CB00014B/3206